If in Him, You Believe

Susan Angus-Perez

NEWMAN SPRINGS PUBLISHING
320 Broad Street
Red Bank, NJ 07701

First originally published by Newman Springs Publishing 2023

ISBN 979-8-89061-194-9 (Paperback)
ISBN 979-8-89061-195-6 (Digital)

Printed in the United States of America

THIS IS A TRUE STORY

*(In strict compliance to privacy and confidentiality laws,
the characters in the story bear fictitious names.)*

CONTENTS

PROLOGUE

Fear thou not; for I am with thee: Be not dismayed; for I am thy God. I will strengthen thee; yes, I will help thee; yea, I will uphold thee with the right hand of my righteousness.

—*Isaiah 41:10 KJV*

What would you do if trials and sufferings knock at your door in waves? How resilient are you in times of distress and ordeals? Have you even gauged your flexibility and preparedness when the rain starts pouring in and never stops? Have you ever wondered whom to ask for assistance if these things occur? Do you have someone who would support you regardless of the circumstance? I'm sure, for the most part, no one is ready for any turmoil to occur in their life ever. And who wants those? We all hope for a happy, perfect life in every way we can, right? Did you ever question yourself about the existence of a powerful Creator? And if you're convinced that there's an omnipotent one up there, do you completely believe in him? Have you ever pondered why you were born on a planet called Earth? What was the main reason why you're here at a designated date and time? For what purpose? Have you ever questioned your life's journey?

Life's journey differs in the sense that it is unique and personal. Your journey is yours and yours alone, and mine is exclusively mine and no one else's. There might be some similarities but never a duplicate. We all have different journeys, different paths along the way. We all were meant to learn some things here on earth, but we're not meant to permanently stay. Our journey together here on earth varies, but we all are bound toward the same destination at the finality of our life. Life is a gift to many. A very precious gift given to mankind. Once I asked a wise man, "What is the meaning of life?"

His soft reply struck me to the deepest core. He said, "Life itself has no meaning. It is an opportunity to create a meaning." His words reverberated me to this day. As I reflected on it, it made me realize that life really is what I make it. In life, my beliefs affect my choices that shape my actions, right? Then my actions determine results. It is I that make my life. Plain and simple. It is I that find ways to know my resolve of why I'm here and, hopefully, will fulfill my purpose as it unfolds. There will be challenges and barriers that will come my way to make life more interesting and, of course, overcoming them is what makes life more meaningful and worth living. We need to remember that some of the most beautiful things we have in life come from our own mistakes committed in the past, whether intentionally or not. Blessings that come into our life also emanate from the trials and tribulations that we face daily. We won't know happiness if there's no misery to conquer. A teardrop is equal to an ounce of laughter, so they say. Hard times are often considered as blessings in disguise.

Don't be intimidated by such. Go out there and conquer them one at a time. Be grateful for your inner strength and unrelenting faith that God has bestowed upon you. Use them well. Use them sensibly. Always remember that your past was never a mistake if you learned from it. Likewise, be wary that life is a gift from above, and the Giver of life allows happiness and pain, success and failures, good and evil for us to experience and to test our faith in him, nonetheless. We choose our action, but we must be sensible of the consequence.

When everything seems to be going against you, just recall that the airplane will take off ground against the wind, not with it. If you feel like you're losing everything, just remember that even trees that are created by God lose their leaves, one way or another and, yet, they remain standing tall and patiently wait for a better weather ahead. Trials and tribulations are likened to storms in different categories that come our way. And once the heavy storm of your life is over, you won't even remember how you conquered it and how you managed to survive. You're not even sure if the storm has already left, but know this: You won't be the same person again once you walked out of it triumphantly. You will be stronger than you think and smarter than what you perceived yourself to be. *The winner takes it all.*

Having said all of these, a very sweet friend of mine enthusiastically and heartily shared with me her life journey for as far as she can recall. Her story was her own, may possibly have similarities with others but not a repeat. Everything was very vivid in her memory. It was surreal. I intently listened to her as she narrated every chapter of her life story, and I gladly wrote it (with her permission, of course) with the intention to share it for everyone to learn a lesson perchance or to experience what I felt while writing this book. I sporadically cried as I penned her life journey. But there were paradoxical moments during the narration where I smiled, then sobbed, and laughed and giggled sometimes. She was all out as the storyteller. I was just her pen and paper when the entire process commenced.

I'm grateful for the opportunity she gave me as I wrote and compiled her story into a manuscript. I had the time of my life listening intently as she unfolded the events one chapter at a time. It was intense yet whimsical. It was powerful yet grounded. Her life story was all about joy of living initially, then transformed into a painful tragedy, followed by unforgiving turns of nightmare events and, eventually, a blissful living. All these are in the chapters ahead. And my friend reminded me to *never* forget to mention who walked with her along the way. And she calls him her heavenly Father.

Enjoy the book, and may her life journey serve as an inspiration and motivation to you as the reader, and allow some reflection on how my friend managed to triumph against all odds in life.

Happy reading.

THE HAPPY MOMENTS

I'll give up anything I own in this world if that's what it takes to go back to those happy childhood days. No money, wealth, earthly possession can delay my wish to be, once more, a little girl, even for just one bright summer day.

—*Susie A. Perez*

She was born to poor, hardworking parents during a chaotic, impoverished period in one of the sparsest cities in a country located in Asia. Accordingly, the day she came into the world, it was awfully dreary, lonely, and eerie. But she was a prize won upon her arrival to the family. Her parents adored her. She was her father's princess, and she was everything a father could want. Wherever her father went, she was there.

Being the middle child and the only girl, Shez was as brilliant and as independent as can be. She knew exactly what she wanted and will get it, regardless. She started her education when she was five as a first-grader in their community school. There were no nursery or kindergarten classes at that time. At a very tender age, she had shown higher intelligence and power, and her impoverished background did not deter her leadership in her classes. She was more mature intellectually than her age, and her parents noticed it as well. Adored by classmates (boys and girls) and teachers, she held the key to success wherever she went. Poor as they were, the parents managed to give Shez the things every little girl dreamed of. Yes, indeed, her name was *Shez*.

Their neighborhood was a haven for Shez. She was loved, cared for, and protected by the people around her. Her humble abode was a paradise in her eyes. All kinds of flowers bloomed in front of their yard, and all types of vegetables draped at the back. They did have a huge balete tree at the backyard, where all the scary, ghostly stories emanated from during storytelling time at their little veranda.

Shez's mother was a great storyteller. Every dusk, all the neighborhood children gathered around the small veranda to listen to Shez's mother tell a story. Be it a fantasy one or a scary version, the thrills and excitement were transparently manifested through their innocent faces. Nights with full moon couldn't deny the neighborhood children from playing in the front yard (9:00 p.m.–10:00 p.m.). It was believed that during those times, magical and enchanted creatures came out from their hiding to play with them. The luminous moonlight added the fairytale madness for all. It was the time to play "hide-and-seek," "water by the line," "Touching Ball," "Ring a Ring o' Roses," "London Bridge," and many other games that were popular at that time. The children's parents happily watched them from their patios and enjoyed the fun as well. The children played until they could play no more. They then cleaned up after themselves and happily hopped into their own warm beds, most likely dreaming of the fun-filled activities they had that day.

On the weekends, Shez, Jazmine (her best friend), and other friends (siblings included) fearlessly climbed trees and hills, just half a mile from their backyard. How they loved to climb the caimito tree and gathered the ripened fruits and pretty much stayed up in the tree as they consumed the fruits with satisfaction. They would then go straight to the singing brook (so they called it) and played until twilight. Shez and friends played with their self-made kites during the weekends. They stayed around the big plaza, near their home, where they played like there was no tomorrow and flew those kites as Mr. Wind gleefully assisted them with their merriment. There were no dull moments with Shez and friends, and they bonded lovingly like family. The singing brook, which was a mile from Shez's home, was their meeting place. This was the place where they swam, washed clothes, chased frogs, tracked dragonflies, and had the best time of their young, little, innocent lives. Shez was known to tuck her collected froggies in the butt, inside her undies, and the laughter was unstoppable from friends who teased her for doing it.

At night, they altogether collected dazzling fireflies, placed them in a big glass jar, and used it as their flashlight in the darkest hours. They played and enjoyed one another from morn till twilight. Problems, worries, concerns were unknown to these kids. They had their own little world that no one knew, except them. The boisterous laughter and loud voices echoed through the entire place that exhibited magical moments where one can only imagine what was going on in every child's imagination. Play was their full-time job at that moment in time. Those were the fun memories of childhood that Shez vividly recalled with fondness.

School days were even sweeter. Everyone shared their snacks/food during recess. And when it rained, they ran around barefoot, splashing every puddle of water they could find. They dived down any murky area and immersed themselves with mud, all over their body. And boy, the fun had only just begun. Using banana leaves as their umbrellas, they sang and danced under the rain until it stopped, until they were soaked, until their lips turned blue, until they saw a rainbow that, for them, signified good luck because they believed there was a pot of gold at the end of it and wished they could reach and pick it up for everyone. They did their homework together, they read their books together; these neighborhood children were always together growing up. Shez was always the top of her class. Gold medals abound in their home. They were displayed at their tiny living room for all to see. Shez's parents beamed with pride with her achievements. She was their diamond in the rough. She was everything to them.

She led her class every year, no doubt about it, and yet she was as humble and carefree and grounded, despite all the attention given to her from classmates, schoolmates, teachers, and parents. Shez had the most medals awarded in academics and in extracurricular activities such as Girl Scouting and many more. She did not excel in math but loved it anyway. She likewise maintained her love for singing and dancing and never hesitated to show it off when requested by the elders.

Shez's older brother, JoJo, was likewise packed with talents, especially in dancing. JoJo was the star dancer in their small elementary school campus. He was always present in dance competitions and collected various awards for such. He was everyone's friend in the neighborhood. He was kind, courteous, respectful, hardworking, and jolly. No wonder the children loved and adored him. Such a great personality.

Holidays, especially Christmas, were the most awaited event in Shez's life. Caroling with her friends was a sweet incentive. Oh, how she loved to sing Christmas songs with everyone. I guess Christmas was her favorite holiday back then. No school. No homework. No books. Nothing but pure fun. Shez and her brothers never missed going to the mangrove to pick out the best tree ever and decorate it with paper toys (since they didn't have any actual toys) and paint it green and white. They made soap bubbles and hardened them under the sun. This to them symbolized snow and playfully slapped the hardened bubbles all over the tree that came from the muddy mangrove not far from where they lived. JoJo made sure that the homemade Christmas tree stayed standing steadily in a big tin can and ready for display in their tiny living room.

JoJo made a star out of bamboo sticks every year and wrapped it with Japanese paper. He carefully placed a little candle inside the hollow bamboo star to light the outside stairway. The lighted star was mesmerizing to watch. It lighted up for Mary and Joseph, that they may find a manger for sweet Jesus. That was the whole meaning of why they had a lighted-with-a-candlestick-star by their stairway. How cool was that? There were a lot of excitement in Shez's household every Christmas. The coming of Santa Claus on Christmas Eve (midnight) was the most talked about among the children in the neighborhood. Each of them held a Christmas wish within their sweet, innocent heart. Each of them wanted to meet Santa in person, very badly. Everyone would like to be in Santa's "good kids" list.

At Shez's household, Mother got busy cooking and baking delicacies and sweets in preparation for the Christmas Eve and, of course, for Christmas day. Too much commotion in the kitchen, the delicious aroma of foods being prepared filled the air. The children singing Christmas carols, and the entire neighborhood was in the mood for the holidays like no other. Unforgettable magical moments that only existed in the hearts of the children living in a rural, quiet, tranquil, quaint community.

Shez's childhood was just an ordinary one. Filled with laughter and tears. Poor as they were, there never was a need for extra happiness and love among them. They had these and eagerly shared it with anyone who wanted extra love and care. It was free after all. The children can readily attest that sharing is loving and loving is sharing. No doubt about it.

THE DEVIL CAME TO TOWN

The devil doesn't come in a red cape and pointed horns. He doesn't deceive or make threats at all. He presents the sweetest personality at first but gets cunning and deceitful when, in his trap, you fall.

—Shez

Shez's happy home was always packed with laughter as the lazy days went by. On one occasion, her father met his best friend from long ago and introduced him to the family. The stranger-friend was welcomed like family, accommodated, fed, and fellowshipped by everyone. He seemed very nice and, according to him, he was happily married with four kids of his own. He felt comfortable with Shez's family, and not for long, he was a constant figure seen in the house. He was often seen conversing with her parents, brought some baked goods and toys for them, and many more. A very kind man indeed, and very slowly, Shez and her brothers noticed even more kind acts from this man.

He appeared to be more conversant with their mother. He was always by her side, talking warmly and animatedly that entertained their mother so much. They laughed and giggled together like teenagers. They talked in whispers. Their body language seemed weird as far as the children noticed. They looked very close as they exchanged soft conversations that were only audible to them. The children saw that and didn't like it. Shez was seven years old at that time, but she was intellectually mature and knew that something was brewing underneath this nonsense. Even Shez's father noted the strange behavior.

"What is going on?" asked Shez's father to his wife one day.

"Nothing," snubbed the wife.

To avoid arguments, Shez's father would leave the house unannounced and would return very late at night, when the children were sound asleep. Shez noticed the presence of this man was unrestrained, especially when her father was at work. He apparently was a constant visitor and companion to her mother. Shez did not like it, but she was just a child. She didn't know what to say or do. She told her brothers about it; nevertheless, the brothers just brushed it off. She felt awkward every time this man came to the house without her father's presence.

What is he doing with mother? was her relentless question to herself.

She was horribly bothered by it, yet her voice was unheard and ignored. And because she was just a little girl, she would just leave and play outside with friends, leaving her mother and the man alone. The impromptu visits swelled quickly. They seemed to be always together. Shez's father worked all day and came home very late at night. The love and laughter that used to fill the household vanished like bubbles from an old, sour wine that was left at the cellar for ages. Shez likewise noted that her father was frequently intoxicated and angry for no apparent reason. Their house was no longer a happy home. Shez's parents clashed almost every day, like cats and dogs. The peaceful living left the family in a slow-motion manner where no one perceived it until it was too late.

There was always a ruckus, shrieking, hollering, and swearing between the parents. Shez's father's behavior changed from being a loving husband and father into an undesirable person almost overnight. He was no longer the well-loved and respected father they used to know. He appeared to have lost his reasons and senses. He abhorred the children, even Shez. He loathed being with the family. He yelled and screamed at them, more so with his wife. He beat and cursed the children for unspecified reasons. He was always inebriated. He detached himself from them in every possible way he could. It was appalling and disgusting. These actions were repeatedly exhibited almost every day. There was no peace and love in the house. Shez and her brothers hated coming home, but they were trapped and had nowhere to go.

Shez ended up spending most of her study hours at Jazmine, her best friend's house. If she could only stay with Jazmine, even for a day or two, she would do it. But she felt obliged to go home and be with her family, regardless of the situation. She felt her presence could at least allay fears and arguments between her parents. She ended up kneeling inside her room to pray every night.

"What has become of my father?" she cried to the Lord. "What is going on with my mother? Why do they fight all the time?" she continued. "*Please, dear Father in heaven, please make the man who disturbed our peace go away,*" she begged. "*Please, heavenly Father, please. I beg thee. Can you please bring back the father that I know and love? Please, dear God, I beg of you. Please!*" She prayed with silent tears rolling down her cheeks.

It was profound. It was overwhelmingly emotional. They say "*a sincere prayer from an innocent child is always heard in heaven.*" But Shez wasn't sure if God really heard her.

The home's negative atmosphere worsened as the days passed. Shez's mother, as always, depended upon her lover during this chaotic time. One of their neighbors reported seeing the mother and her boyfriend meeting up by the woods, located close to their backyard. There were tall trees and thick bushes in that area, and they rendezvoused there each time the children were in school and the husband was at work. A complete insanity! Indeed! What happened to their mother? Why was she behaving immorally? Why? Why? Why? The close-knit neighborhood disbanded, and gossip went a flying all around like a ball of fire. The ugly rumors traveled quicker than the strike of lightning, faster than the terrifying sound of a thunderstorm. The situation was unmanageable, disconcerting on the part of the children, infuriating, sickening, and distasteful. Worse, it was immoral, and the children were not shielded from it.

Shez's mother didn't care a bit about the gossip against her. She stoically supported her lover. She expressed her feelings to Shez and her brothers that she was ready to separate from their father. The mother further verbalized that her love for their father had gone awry. "There's nothing in here"—she pointed to her heart—"for him anymore. There's no more room for him. Period."

The children were flabbergasted at their mother's demeanor. They were all dumbfounded.

"She isn't thinking right!" whispered JoJo to his siblings as they cautiously walked away from her.

Their mother was verbal. No reservation whatsoever. She wanted her freedom. She was ready to leave her family for her lover. It was agonizing and painful for the children, especially for Shez. Her little innocent heart was full of anguish and despair. She felt betrayed by her mother. She felt neglected, unloved, abandoned, and uncared for. The feeling of uncertainty and insecurity wrapped around their used-to-be-happy home. The abundance of love and laughter turned into an unending nightmare. The situation appeared endless and broken. It looked like the light at the end of the tunnel was nowhere. It was impossible to find. So unreachable and so far away.

The negativity of their household continued like forever. The suffering of the children seemed endless. Shez's mother continued seeing her lover. Nocturnal meetings ensued. Secret places were discovered. Numerous hidden rendezvous were abundant. The adultery and immorality of these two consenting souls persisted. A huge mistake. A big humiliation to the entire family, most especially to Shez's father. Shez herself wanted to confront her mother. She had so many questions in her mind. But how? How can a seven-year-old girl confront a parent? She did not know how. Poor Shez. She ended up kneeling before their altar, praying for assistance. Crying uncontrollably, weeping bitterly, sobbing sullenly—her heart was shattered and fragmented.

The saddest thing was no one dared comfort her. Not even her brothers. For the first time in her life, she felt so alone and lonely. Her friends noticed her behavior, her teachers knew what was happening at her home. But not one of them was brave enough to console her. Not one reassured her. Not one of the teachers was valiant enough to investigate what was happening in Shez's home. They were all left stunned. They were all shocked. They most likely didn't know what to say or do. And so the saga in Shez's family hounded.

Shez's turmoil turned for the worst when her father started abusing her mother verbally, physically, and even mentally. I guess these abuses occurred out of frustration on the part of the father. Almost every day of their existence, Shez's father would literally hit his wife with his fist. He kicked and cursed her in front of the children. It was a maddening memory as Shez cried while she continued telling me her life story. I cried with her a lot. There were times that I found it difficult to concentrate on writing since some of the past events she disclosed were disheartening.

One evening, Shez and her brothers were in the kitchen, quietly having a simple dinner that was prepared by their mother. Peacefully and reverently, they enjoyed the modestly prepared food while exchanging an interesting conversation regarding school activities. It seemed like a pleasant moment to savor when, suddenly, Shez's father bolted from the front door that literally scared them all to death. He was severely intoxicated and held a .45 caliber pistol as he ordered everyone to stand up by the kitchen sink. He was dead serious as he pointed the gun at his wife's face. The children were horrified at the scene. Shez wanted to cry but couldn't. She was frozen and speechless. Fortunately, the father slowly walked away from them and quietly settled himself on the couch and slept with a gun in his hand. Disgusted at her father's behavior, she started hating him secretly. It was a day to remember as far as Shez was concerned. The family was no more. The unit was ominously broken and shattered. At this point, Shez just wanted to run away from it all.

The love was gone. The respect flew out of the window. Her father was always drunk for most days. Her mother found comfort and solace in the arms of her lover. The children were neglected. The unit was factually disbanded. Broken. Dispersed. It was absurdity. It was painful. The children lost the respect and love for the parents. There was never peace and happiness in their dwelling place. All these vanished in a snap of a finger. Sad. So sad. The family was ruthlessly attacked by the devil in a hushed and cunning way. Devious. Tricky. It started so innocuously. The devil presented himself as a good friend and, yet, coveted someone else's wife without reservation. No remorse at all of what was going on inside that once-upon-a-time-happy and harmonious family. What could have gone wrong? Why was this loving family vulnerable to such? Were they destined to suffer like this? Where was God when this inconceivable thing struck? So many questions dominated Shez's mind as she stood in silence.

She even wished to end her young life, but she didn't know how. She just wanted to run away, away from it all, away from ill gossip, opinions, and mockeries, away from the world. She felt like she could not handle the situation anymore. Of all the siblings, Shez was the one most stricken by the existing home condition. She became very emotional. She lost her love for learning. She didn't care if she was in the honor roll or not. Who cares? Nobody! The world was a sham. The people around her (who used to be loving and caring) seemed like robots or puppets who didn't sympathize or empathize with her. *Everyone's a fake.*

The beatings continued for quite a long time. Shez's mother was a picture of a battered woman whose body was covered with black-and-blue, all the time. Terrifying cries from the children could be heard around the neighborhood, but nobody came to the rescue. The entire community was mum about the horrendous setting. Regrettably, there was no such thing as domestic violence at that time. During that era, the father was the head of the family (respected, obeyed, loved) and pretty much could do anything (good or bad) to his family, and it was accepted by society. That was the way of life before.

One fateful night, the unthinkable happened. Shez's father caught his wife and the lover in the act. Immediately, the coward lover ran away from the situation. Shez's mother was thrown out of the family's house, like instantly. She ended up going back to her side of the family that lived in another city. She was abruptly separated from the children who cried a river, but the father stuck to his decision to let her go. Right after the separation, once again, there was peace in the home. The father stopped drinking and took care of the children as a single parent. Shez's grandfather (father's side) came to live with the family and helped take care of the children. Finally, there was a quiet and peaceful atmosphere within the home for a long season.

A few months later, Shez and her brothers started missing their mother profoundly. They desperately wanted her back. They strongly verbalized their longing to be with their mother. They wanted her back. Period. Shez's father, with great hesitancy, eventually went to his wife's family and begged her to come back. The wife was hesitant but secretly longed for her children.

"Come home. The children need you badly. They miss you so much," he lamented. "Let's forget what happened. Let's start a new life and be a happy family once more," he continued.

It took at least three days to finally convince his wife to come home. Once again, the forlorn house transformed into a happy home in Shez's eyes. She was beyond grateful. Oh, how she loved her mother. She was so delighted, and once again, she was back to her old form, happy, on top of her class, participated in all school activities, played with Jazmine and others, like nothing happened. She was on top of the world. Her father, once again, reverted into his normal self. He was loving, family-oriented, and sweet with a ready smile and laughter that exuded in his face. Her grandfather decided to go back to his province since Shez's mother returned home. Again, the family was intact or, at least, it looked like it.

A family unit is from *God*. It should be a refuge from any storm. It should be the greatest support to the members of the unit. Evil and wickedness will never win if the family stays in love, bonded, united, and prays together. God will safeguard them from any tragedy or iniquity if they are united with an unfading faith and full trust in *him*.

A SHOT FIRED

Playing with fire on either side of a relationship can be fatal.
It creates a mayhem to everyone involved in the family unit.
Once the fire is started, it may be impossible to put out,
and the consequences therein can be more than lethal.

—Chito Barrios

A few months passed, and the family continuously lived quietly and harmoniously in their home. The family involved themselves with many outdoor activities, much to Shez's delight. There was an event where they rode on a pump boat that took them to a nearby isolated island for fun. That place was very memorable for Shez. It was there that they really bonded and enjoyed one another. The white sandy beach, the food, the camaraderie, the lazy warm weather, the picnic, the games— so unforgettable. They had the time of their lives in moving pictures. The happiness was indescribable. Endless laughter. Good food. Fun. Fun. Fun. There was a time, likewise, when the entire family attended the next town fiesta celebration. They stayed with relatives for a couple of days and enjoyed the aura and atmosphere of the community's festival. Shez and JoJo had the opportunity to showcase their talents for dancing and singing with other children, and it was well-received and applauded by the people.

The family watched movies and live entertainment together. They enjoyed one another, and their faces glowed with peace and contentment as they navigated the chaotic world as a family. Yes, there was love within the unit once again. There was a commitment and respect as they looked forward to the future with concerns and doubts, and yet they had each other, and that was sure enough to navigate and face uncertainties and ambiguities as they moved on to the next chapter of their life.

The routine family schedule was back into their simple yet happy life when the school season opened. Shez and her friends were busy with pre-school preparations. They shopped for school supplies together, covered their free books and notebooks, and sharpened their pencils. Shez even got a couple of new cheap beautiful school dresses. Her father got her a pair of new sneakers and a pair of off-white lacey socks. She was on cloud nine. She would be in grade 4 at this time (and would be turning nine years old in a few months). Excitement was in the air for these young guns. Shez, Jazmine, and friends already had plans of sleepovers to do homework together. Such a fun group to belong to.

Her mother got her a nice sky-blue-colored school bag. What a blessing. Shez was endlessly grateful. Shez and friends spent their time studying and playing together. Jazmine spent countless sleepovers at her house to study and do homework and vice versa. Shez and Jazmine were inseparable since the first grade. They just loved each other like sisters. They fought occasionally, but the hurt feelings disappeared rapidly. They were destined to be buddies and pals. Yes, indeed, two peas in a pod. That was exactly what they were.

School had been an adventure for Shez and Jazmine and other friends. There were various competitions and contests that they all participated in. Prices were won. They could be material or cash, but the fact that they won made them brighter and bigger stars on the small elementary campus. They belonged to a popular group in school, and they loved it. Scouting class was matchless. It was their favorite extracurricular activity. They met every Friday after classes. They wore their Brownie uniforms, held a whistle in their hands, wore a dwarflike hat, and a brown belt around their cute, slim waists. Their well-polished black shoes were noticeably clean and neat. The activities in the Scouting class were a treat and an adventure for the girls. The laughter resounded within the campus like a roaring lion. The games were unparalleled. No one wanted to miss out on Scouting. No one.

But somewhere down the road, the happiness and contentment of this family was cut short. It happened so fast. Unknown to many, Shez's mother continued seeing her lover in secret. It was a clandestine affair that no one knew. They were very vigilant. Cautious. Cunning. Their relationship was even stronger. Full of illicit passion. Full of licentious desire. Why was Shez's mother so eccentrically in love with her lover? Was it love? Or was it just lust? How could she betray her loving husband who adored her and the loving children? What was she thinking? Meticulous as they were, an innocent bystander spotted them in a secluded location making love. It was weird. The nervous eyewitness, who knew Shez's family, quietly revealed the facts to a neighbor about what he saw. The news mutely scattered within the entire neighborhood like wildfire. Everyone knew, except the involved family. Everyone in that serene, quaint community was shocked and stunned at what was going on. It was the breaking news that never stopped. It was the hottest topic of the day. Every day!

Shez suspected all along what was going on. She remained mum and reserved. She didn't know what to do. She wanted to tell her father, but she was so scared of the consequence. Even her best friend Jazmine was aware but didn't have the guts to tell Shez. And Shez most likely thought that Jazmine already knew. It was a topic both had avoided during casual conversations. It must have been disappointing. It must have been heartbreaking for Shez.

"Here we go again," she softly whispered to herself.

Their home atmosphere, once again, reverted into a cold, violent house of terror. Shez's father went back to his old habits of alcohol and the no-care-attitude. The beatings toward their mother restarted. A river of tears was sadly shed by the children. They once again felt hopeless and neglected. The case was doomed. This time, Shez prayed that her parents would just separate. There were times that she wished her mother dead. She was so frustrated. She eventually changed her attitude concerning the home front. Shez decided that she'd maintain her happy disposition at all times, be it at home, in school, with friends, and within the neighborhood. She refused to be influenced by the struggles at home anymore. She decided to be her usual self, regardless—happy, hopeful, optimistic, bubbly, and energetic in the middle of her family's unfathomable dilemma. Most of her time was spent with her best friend, Jazmine. She felt comforted and loved when she was with her good friend. Her fourth-grade teacher, occasionally, showered some motherly affection and love that made her a solace for a heartbroken little girl. There were times when Shez imagined having her fourth-grade teacher as her real mother.

"She was loving and caring," according to Shez when asked why she adored her teacher. "I wished she was my mother," she shyly admitted.

The situation at home became worst as days passed. There was no resolution in plain sight. There was no hope for appeasement. A conflict was declared. Pride versus pride. Evil versus evil. Horrible yet possible. They didn't care about the children. All they cared about was their own selfish, arrogant, condescending selves. What a pity! The children sought comfort and peace from their own friends and teachers. That was all they could do. They continued their daily routine amidst the dispute between their parents.

One significant afternoon, Shez's family was home, and for the first time in their sad life, silence and stillness overwhelmed the entire house. It felt eerie, as if there was a ticking timebomb ready to explode. It felt wicked, according to Shez. She thought evil attacked them, and it was inside their abode and winning. Shez's ill feeling was overwhelming. The scene at that time was Shez's father was cleaning his .45 caliber pistol in the living room (he was a military), Mother was preparing dinner, JoJo, the oldest, was with their father as he helped him clean the firearm, while the other siblings were in the backyard, fixing their toy car, and Shez was preparing for a bath. When, out of the blue, a gun fired! *A shot was fired*! Just once, and this made Shez's heartbeat stop for a second.

"*What's happening in the living room?*" was her inquiry to herself.

The siblings immediately rushed to the living area and found their mother lying helplessly on the floor, bathed in her own blood. Shocked, Shez didn't know what to do. How could she? She was only eight years old. Her siblings instantly summoned their neighbors for assistance. Everyone in the neighborhood came to the rescue, and right before Shez's eyes, she saw her mother wrapped in a blanket and was quickly transported to the nearest hospital. Her father accompanied his wife, and her other siblings were nowhere to be found. Shez was left unattended as she sobbed immensely. She was senseless. She was sickened. She was beside herself until Jazmine arrived and embraced her tightly. Now both were crying silently yet desperately. It was a horrific scene. The devil's wish finally came true. *Evil had won.*

That very evening, Shez, together with her siblings, found themselves sleeping behind bars, together with their father. He was under arrest.

"Why are we sleeping here?" Shez asked JoJo, who seemed oblivious to what was happening.

"I don't know" replied her oldest brother.

"Possibly accompanying Father?" the other brother retorted.

Shez lay down on the hard, cold wooden bed with no blanket on, beside her brothers. She was mum. Her tears continued in stillness.

This is a nightmare. Please wake me up! I'm having a nightmare. Shez kept pinching herself. *I'm having a very bad dream. Somebody, please wake me up!*

She wordlessly pleaded to anyone who could hear her. She prayed hard to her heavenly Father. Sad to say, she was indeed having a nightmare in a reality setting. From the far-right corner of the cell, she saw her father wept quietly as he asked for forgiveness and mumbled indecipherable words that only he could comprehend. The children soundlessly left him alone. They didn't bother or talk to him. They gave him his space as he reflected on the events that quickly unfolded earlier that day. Pretty soon, Shez fell asleep. Tired. Hungry. Cold. Lonely. Motherless. She cried herself to sleep. Poor Shez!

The following miserable day, her mother's body was brought to their home after being embalmed. For the first time once again, Shez saw her mother's lifeless body inside a casket. The mother looked sad yet undisturbed in her white dress. She looked like she was just asleep.

"Is she just asleep? Will she wake up soon?" Shez asked JoJo.

She gathered no response. Shez noticed a rosary was intertwined between her mother's fingers, and she had makeup on. Shez couldn't stop crying. Ditto with her brothers. It was a day of lamentation. A terrible day of mourning. Grief and sadness enveloped the children. It was a moment of gloom that only the children could openly express their inner feelings to the whole world without uncertainty, without hesitation.

The neighborhood rallied behind the family. They all pitched in with the family's needs. Their assistance was overpowering. Once again, they had shown and manifested the loving spirit of the community. The neighbors took care of the children. They fed, consoled, comforted, and supported them. Shez's father remained behind bars while the neighbors prepared the burial of the body in the Catholic way. Shez's maternal relatives from a faraway city came after they were notified of the unexpected passing. Her mother was only thirty-six years old when her life was taken away.

A pandemonium broke out when Shez's mother's family arrived. The entourage was intense. A bunch of them bullied the entire neighborhood. They wanted to take the body with them. They screamed, cried, and cursed everyone present in the house where the body was laid. It was quite a spectacle. An unpleasant scene. Fortunately, despite their intimidation and harassment, the dead body remained in the house and would be interred as planned in the resting place, just a couple of miles away from home. Shez's mother's family, especially the oldest sister, was so upset that she destroyed belongings found in Shez's house. She went wild. She expressed vengeance. She wanted to kill Shez's father. She was beside herself, and her rage could not be contained. But can you blame her? I believe she had all the right to be angry and furious at the very moment. The neighbors gave space to Shez's maternal side of the family. They politely left the house and allowed them to grieve in their own way. And that was that. An unthinkable, unimaginable thing sadly happened to this poor family. The tragedy was surreal. The life of the affected members of the family would never be the same after this. Most especially Shez.

She never realized that she was predestined for an adventure of a lifetime that only she and she alone could tackle. Shez placed her unrelenting faith in God. She just knew that God would never abandon or neglect her. God always was and is on her side. She felt his love all along. She knew that only God could protect her and would love her unconditionally until the end of the world, until eternity. She just knew it from the bottom of her heart. *And that knowledge kept her comforted as she faced the cruel world head-on.*

KIDNAPPED

Kidnapped victims may suffer a long-term effect in the deepest consciousness of their soul. It can destroy their sense of thinking and decision-making, which can agonize the very core.

—*Susie A. Perez*

Shez was behind bars together with her father when she felt the need to meet her mother's family. So Shez asked her father's permission if she could go home. Initially, the father did not approve it. He wanted the children not to be involved with the nuisances that were exhibited by his wife's family. But Shez was determined to go home to meet them; so, ultimately, her father consented. Little did the father know that was the last time he'd see his daughter's innocent face. Shez gave him a reassuring hug and a peck on his cheek as she bade him adieu. They lovingly embraced each other as Shez whispered into her father's ear with "I'll see you later "—and warmly, she went her way.

She waved her father goodbye as he saw her disappear from his view. One eager step at a time, she wanted to see her aunties and uncles. She yearned for their love and attention. She hoped that they'd give her some money so she could buy her favorite candy bar when she got a chance. Her mother's family remained in their house, grieved, and wondered why the children were nowhere to be found. They wanted to see them. They asked the neighbors but, unfortunately, they mustered no response. Shez walked quite a distance from the prison building to her home. Big beads of sweat were seen dripping from her innocent face as she slowly strode herself under the scorching heat of the sun. She was exhausted and starved, plus she didn't get to sleep well the night before. At this time, her brothers were nowhere to be seen.

Where could they be? she wondered.

Once again, she felt deserted and separated. But she remained optimistic and hopeful. She was quite thrilled to finally see her relatives from the maternal side. She heard a lot of good stories about them from her mother. This time, she double-paced herself, despite her shaky physical condition. She was awfully starved. Unmindful of the blazing sun, she eventually ran toward home. She certainly couldn't wait to see them to feel their love and attention, just as every little girl longed for.

Her aunties and uncles were so glad to see her. They hugged her and wept together, beside her mother's casket. It was an extremely emotional reunion between Shez and her relatives. It was an endearing scene. Love was transparently manifested among them. It was tender. Exactly what Shez hoped and prayed for. She was grateful for the warm reception she received from her mother's relatives, especially her Auntie Mary (the oldest among her mother's siblings). Her Aunt Mary held her hand the whole time. She was not let go. She was held lovingly yet tightly and firmly. Shez didn't mind at all. After all, she was her auntie. She felt like she had a provisional mother at that very moment. And she enjoyed the attention given to her. She decided to remain with them as they all grieved together.

Time quickly passed, and Shez found herself still with her relatives, and this time, they took her inside a nice car. She thought that they were just driving around to pass the hour away from the awful situation. But not all of them were with her inside the car. Her Auntie Mary and the rest were left behind. It was just her auntie Em and Uncle Patrick, together with the driver, who stayed vigilantly with her. At first, Shez was puzzled, but being a little girl, she didn't put much thought to it. She was having a great time. She was loved, fed, comforted, and reassured. So who cared as to where they were bound? They drove for hours (and speeding) until Shez fell asleep on her auntie Em's lap. Hours passed, and Shez woke up only to find out that she was in another place, another environment, with different scenes. She was in awe. What a beautiful city. She had no idea that she was intentionally kidnapped.

So this was my mother's city, she concluded when she found out where she was at.

She was mesmerized. She was overjoyed. She was welcomed by many cousins that she didn't know before. She was very happy to finally meet and know them. Immediately, Shez felt so at home and had the time of her life. Shez was on cloud nine. She forgot her loved ones she left behind. Her lost brothers. Her helpless father. They most likely already found out that she was missing. Seriously. All she cared was that she was very happy, playing with her cousins. There were so many of them, and they all looked her age. Momentarily, she was filled with laughter and giggles, together with cousins who embraced her as their own sibling. She was all over the place with them. She thought that this could be her second home. Her second family.

On the other hand, Shez's absence was already markedly noted by the neighbors. They were all alarmed and worried. The bad news reached Shez's father, and immediately, he was released from the cell to find his daughter. At this point, the entire neighborhood was out looking for her. Shez's father contacted the military to assist him. Military trucks were used to find the missing little girl. Somebody from the neighborhood witnessed the fact that Shez was transported into a private car, together with some relatives from the maternal side. Thus, military personnel were dispersed to another city to get hold of her. Once again, it was pandemonium! Chaos crept into the small town, and the residents were in a panic mode, except for Shez's Auntie Mary and other relatives who were left behind. They calmly stayed by the casket's side, not talking. Not reacting. Unremorseful. Untouched by the confusion and turmoil that were enveloping the little community. Shez's father and siblings were desperate and frantic to find her. They were in tears. They were in agony. Extremely worried.

The military found Shez's relatives' residence in the faraway city. They immediately did their search with a warrant in their hands.

"Shez! Shez! Are you here?" They looked around in every nook and cranny of the house. They were armed and focused on their mission, their mission of taking Shez back where she belonged. Unfortunately, they didn't find her. They searched high and low for hours, but there was no Shez.

Where could she be? was the consistent inquiry on their puzzled minds.

They searched until there was no more room to search. Anger and frustration occurred since they simply could not locate the little girl. And, yes! Where could she be?

Unknown to everyone, Shez was taken by her relatives and hid her up in the mountainside of another town. Innocent Shez was kidnapped! And she was clueless that she was taken away from her father and siblings. All the while, she thought she was just there for a visit or something. She didn't know that she wouldn't see her immediate family anymore. Shez, being as naive as she was, just followed along. She obeyed all the orders that her relatives gave her without questions. She was scared and didn't know what to do. So she just played along and remained calm during the ordeal. Little did she know, very little did she know, there was more turmoil and misery lined up ahead of her sad and lonely journey.

After a couple of weeks or so, the relatives found out that the coast was clear and the search was called off. They took Shez out of the hiding and brought her back to the house of her Auntie Mary who was waiting for her (the burial apparently was over).

Auntie Mary exclaimed with glee, "You are now my daughter! You can call me Mama. Lizette (Mary's adopted daughter) is now your older sister. You will obey her and always keep her company."

Shez was stunned yet calm and collected. Lizette was a few years older than Shez, about seven years ahead of her. Shez didn't like Lizette. She appeared spoiled and controlling. Her smile was devilish. Shez managed to nod her little head to show agreement and conformity. Shez liked her other cousins who lived down the road from her Auntie Mary's house. They were almost the same age as she was. She longed to play with them versus staying with Lizette. There was just something about Lizette. And she felt it the first time she met her.

A few weeks passed, Shez was alone in Lizette's bedroom when she heard a big commotion outside. She instantly jumped from the bed and peeped through a small window facing the street. To her dismay, she saw one of her grand-aunties running naked in the street. She saw the neighbors chasing her grand-auntie, shouting, *"Stay away from her! She has gone mad! She's harmful!"*

The neighborhood children started to run after her as well. All of them were chanting, *"Lock her up! Lock her up!"*—as they laughed and, at the same time, screamed at her. Shez felt so sorry for her grand-auntie who indeed had gone mad and mentally broken. Her other relatives who were present at that time started to run after her to keep her safe from others. A long chase ensued within the neighborhood, and the mad woman was finally caught, tied up, and was brought into Mary's house where Shez was hiding in the bedroom. Shez witnessed everything that had transpired, which added to her traumatic experience. She cried and cried and was so scared of the unknown. It was like a horror movie that came alive right in front of her innocent eyes. This occurrence made her relatives very unhappy, especially her Auntie Mary. It was a horrifying scene. The mad woman was finally brought to the hospital for help and was eventually admitted in the mental hospital.

More weeks passed. Shez was already seen as a permanent resident and a member of Mary's family. Shez chose not to call her Mama. She just couldn't. They were all extremely nice and accommodating to her. They bought her some new clothes, shoes, bag, and she was fed delicious, expensive foods that she had not eaten before. She had the time of her life when playing with her cousins. Shez missed school for a few weeks now. She didn't mind at all. She appeared to be happy where she was. On several occasions, she felt nostalgic about her father and siblings. She missed them. She wanted to go home but was quite afraid of telling her Auntie Mary about it. She cried herself to sleep secretly at night and showed a happy face when she was with them. Oh, how she missed her father and brothers. She felt insecure, most of the time, while she tried her best to be of good behavior.

Shez missed school for many weeks now, and she was anxious about it. Her Auntie Mary snapped that it was her father's fault for not forwarding the transcript of records to them. Shez needed the official transcript of records to be enrolled or registered into a new school. Her Auntie Mary blamed Shez's father for everything. Brainwashing is easy, especially when it's done to a vulnerable, naive little girl like Shez. Slowly, she found herself leaning toward staying with her auntie for good. Her longing of going back to her immediate family dwindled. Shez was so confused. She prayed about it but felt like God had abandoned her. Contradictory feelings crept into her innocent thoughts as she comforted herself with beautiful memories of that once-upon-a-time-happy family.

She often dreamed of her father and siblings. Her mind and spirit yearned for home, but she was physically paralyzed to tell anyone about it. Nobody seemed to listen. All she heard were bad things about her father. They all badmouthed him daily. They all brainwashed her slowly yet surely. Overwhelmed, Shez would turn around and cried for hours. No one was there for her frustrations. No one! At this point, Shez terribly missed Jazmine and her other friends from her previous school. She missed the usual activities and the entire neighborhood. She missed her previous life. Poor Shez!

I should have stayed with my father and my brothers. I should have. They were my immediate family. I should have followed my heart for all to see. But I was just a scared child who was brainwashed by the people I trusted. So sad to think the trust given was awfully betrayed.

—Shez

Meanwhile, Shez's father hired a lawyer who could help him retrieve Shez from his deceased wife's relatives. Her father moved heaven and earth to get his daughter back. Shez's grandfather (her father's dad) sold the farm to have enough money to pay for the lawyer. The entire community rallied behind Shez's father. They did their share of fundraising to augment the financial support. Everyone pitched in. They all wanted Shez back. She belonged to them. Not to those bullies from another city. She was well-loved in her old neighborhood. Her friends, especially Jazmine, wanted her back, regardless.

Shez's living condition had become quite stressful for a little girl to bear. Her Auntie Mary brought her to a lawyer's office, one day, without telling her why. She faced an interrogation session with the lawyer that made her quiver and tremble.

"What did I do?" she asked herself.

She obviously didn't know what to say or do. Her maternal relatives geared her up to be the star witness against her own father. They wanted her to be on their side. Shez had no issues to tell her side of the story. The truth of the matter was that she didn't witness the event. She wasn't physically present when the tragedy occurred. She was preparing for bath when it ensued. Hence, she didn't know what happened. She didn't know the truth. She wasn't there. Shez was as confused as can be since her Auntie Mary and other relatives were counting on her to be the star witness. A lot of pressure fell on her shoulder, and she was quite disgusted about it.

"Was this the reason why they took me without my father's consent?" she asked herself softly.

Naive as she was, at the time, she never thought of being used by the relatives to take revenge against her father. She didn't know the true story why her mother died. Was it her father's fault? Was it planned? Was it intentional? Was it murder? Or was it completely a tragic accident? *Who knows?* Shez never knew. She wasn't on the scene. What will she do now? The relatives depended on her. She was in the biggest dilemma of her life. She was torn between two rocks. She just wanted to go away, but how?

On a positive note, Shez's birthday came, and her relatives celebrated the day with a bang. She was finally and officially nine years old. They prepared food and cake with balloons, much to Shez's delight. She spent her special day happily playing with her cousins from across the street. For a moment, she forgot the sadness she felt the previous weeks. She felt very special and loved by everyone. She got many presents from aunties and uncles and cousins. She was delighted and appreciative. She felt a sense of belonging to her mother's clan, and a sense of peace encircled her person. She literally forgot her father and siblings that day. She was in cloud nine the entire day, surrounded by all good things a little girl could dream of. She never had this kind of birthday celebration back then. She never had a birthday cake and balloons, up until now. She never had many birthday presents in her life before. One could see the glow on her face with happiness. She was very thankful.

The feeling of euphoria was short-lived for Shez. Once again, she was brought into the lawyer's office to face more interrogation. The lawyer was kind and friendly yet intimidating. His questions were direct to the point, leaving Shez fearful on how to be truthful. Her Auntie Mary wanted her to be on their side. She wanted Shez's father punished for what he had done. That was the goal. Shez was a smart girl. She knew what her Auntie Mary wanted. She knew what her other relatives wanted. She was aware why they treated her so well. She finally knew why she was snatched and brought to their place. Why she was hidden in a secluded place up in the mountains, for weeks, where no one could find her. She realized their intentions. She had no escape at that time. She needed to just go along with it. Shez was eventually coached to tell lies about the tragedy. She pretended she was there when it happened. She responded to the lawyer's questions in favor to what Mary wanted to hear. The lawyer and her relatives were delighted.

"We have a good case. This girl is our star witness," snapped the criminal attorney.

Boom. Shez wanted to die. The consequences of telling lies were surreal. She didn't expect that the result was fatal and disastrous. She simply didn't know! Shez spent so many sleepless nights after the deceptions she told the lawyer. Her guilty feelings plagued her. She was so inundated with shame and fear. She felt being emitted to an oblivion, like a meteor thrown to an infinite vast sky, and the destination was to nowhere. She was in shambles, and the only thing that could help her get out of this unfortunate circumstance was to tell the truth and nothing but the truth. And, once again, the clueless nine-year-old turned to her heavenly Father for guidance. She cried herself to sleep almost every night. Silently. Remorsefully! Frustratingly! She planned to escape from them, but she didn't know how.

"What will happen to my father after all these false disclosures?" a troubled little girl questioned herself worriedly.

This question haunted her consistently. Occasionally, she assumed punishment was upon her. She was a bad girl. She was beyond control with grief. She longed for home but felt falsely imprisoned in the house of torture and horror. She was helpless, alone, and naive. Why was this girl placed in this extremely volatile situation with no help? She was indeed at the wrong place and time. As a child, she should be with her father and brothers who loved and adored her so much. Why was she tortured and tormented by her relatives from the maternal side? Had she done a grievous act that she was treated inhumanely? And we must remember, she was only nine years old. This was her biggest nightmare that she couldn't wake up. It was tough to be motherless and fatherless at the same time. There was no unconditional love offered to her. Everything has a price to be won.

She was reprimanded to behave this way, talk that way, be this way or else! She wasn't herself anymore. As a matter of fact, she was lost as to who she was. She was a robot who was programmed what to say and how to behave. No one seemed to care for her. No one appeared to love her. No one to turn to but herself. She was indeed sucked into an unbearable and terrifying world where isolation and brainwashing were her company. She was badly traumatized and broken.

A few more weeks passed when Mary received a summons from Shez's city's courthouse. A habeas corpus was served that requested the presence of Shez to report in the courtroom. The habeas corpus was obviously filed by Shez's father. Mary panicked. She didn't want to return the little girl to the rightful parent. She wanted the little child for herself, for her own wicked purpose and vengeance against the remaining parent. Once again, all the relatives joined forces to brainwash this child. They used all the tricks to make Shez choose them instead. She was showered with gifts, delicious foods, conditional love, and more so with fear. All of these made Shez dread them. She was so scared to offend them, especially her Auntie Mary. She wanted to please her all the time to feel the love she longed for in return.

What an unimaginable scenario this was for a nine-year-old. She was indeed torn between right and evil. She was at a crossroad that made her perplexed as to which way to trod on. She was overwhelmingly brainwashed that she stayed quiet and obedient to everything they told her.

The important time came when Mary and other relatives had to take the little girl to the courthouse in Shez's city. The lawyer came with them, all bully-like and cocky, except Shez whose cold, clammy little hand was tightly held by Mary.

She kept whispering to Shez to not make any eye contact with her father once in court. "You do not look at him, by all means! You avoid any conversation with your siblings as well."

Shez hesitantly nodded as a sign of fear and total obedience.

The lawyer piggybacked the order with "When we say you cry, you better cry as loud as you can."

Once again, Shez nodded reluctantly, although baffled about what was really happening. She felt the grip of Mary's hand toward her little wrist went tighter. Her cousin Lizette was there too. Quiet yet arrogant. She acted like Shez's older sister who gave orders to the little girl without reservation. Entering the courtroom was like dying slowly on Shez's part. She saw her siblings. They smiled at her. She responded with a soft grin. She felt delighted inside. Her little heart went thumping so fast. Then she saw an emaciated, pale-looking, old man by her siblings' side. Her father. *There's my papa!* Shez exclaimed to herself.

She was so elated to see them all yet very scared and nervous. She wanted to run toward them and hug them with all her might, but she couldn't. She was paralyzed. Frozen. Fear shrouded her entire being. She was powerless, detached, and totally devoid. Her father looked at her with an extremely lonely face. His eyes were swollen. Shez avoided eye contact as instructed. She felt that she was thrown into an extinction by wicked people that surrounded her like fiery dragons. She felt helpless! Defenseless! Weak!

The trial started. The judge sat on his bench and briefly reviewed the purpose of the case. Lawyers from both sides started arguing and debating. Shez could hardly comprehend them, but Lizette interpreted the conversation for her. The arguments went back and forth until the judge gave the verdict.

"The girl has to be with the father," the judge declared, followed by a sound of a gavel from his table.

Immediately, Mary triggered Shez's hand and stared at her fiercely like a red-eyed devil. "Cry as loud as you can. Now!" she strictly demanded.

The fearful little girl bawled out loudly, and that created an uproar inside the courtroom. The surprised judge looked at the child and spoke one more time and exclaimed, "The girl can stay with the aunt." Final verdict.

Mary, the lawyer, and other relatives instantly took Shez out of the courtroom and out of sight. Shez's father and siblings were left speechless. They were flummoxed. Stunned! *What just happened?* Her father supposedly won her over, but the verdict was reversed, and the final verdict was given. The people's court had spoken. And it should be respected. Shez, on the other hand, was frightened and devastated. She didn't realize that she was totally handed over to her Auntie Mary versus her father. Mary now had the power to control her like her own. She was made a legal guardian to Shez by order of the court. Shez was distraught. Suddenly, she remorsefully sobbed inside the hotel room where they stayed during the trial. She was comforted by Lizette. Shez wanted to go home to her family and pleaded with them to let her go. All the crying, sobbing, and pleading were ignored. Totally disregarded.

Little did she know her father was a complete wreck with a broken heart. He wanted his daughter, but the unpredictable turn of events had gone awry. Why did he lose the case? Why wasn't he rewarded custody for his only daughter? He's the biological father after all. Shez's father was beside himself of the catastrophes that were slowly evolving right before his eyes. Shez's other siblings were quiet and hurt. Why did Shez betray them? Why did she choose Auntie Mary over them? They were oblivious as to what happened to Shez on the other side of the family. She was brainwashed, guarded like a prisoner, bullied, and controlled by heartless, wicked monsters. Shez was in a grim situation. She wanted to go home, but she did not know how.

Several months passed. Shez was already enrolled in a new school. Her father reluctantly permitted her previous school to transfer the transcripts of records. Shez had begun her fourth grade enthusiastically. She was excited meeting new friends, new teachers, and a new environment. She was thrilled. Gradually forgetting where she came from, Shez retained her worries and loneliness at the back burner. She desperately wanted to excel in school. She wanted to do exceptionally well to show her relatives that she was good enough for them. She focused her efforts like a microscope in terms of academics. She was very aware that her Auntie Mary was her financial support, and she wanted to show her that she was very much worth it. Her behavior remained guarded. She was extra careful with her actions and words at the new abode and even at her new school. She met good friends and classmates, but no one compared to her best friend, Jazmine. She loved her new teachers and the new school itself. It was just a half kilometer away by foot, and the best part was she got the opportunity to get away from the house of torture, even for just a few hours in a day.

Shez was, sadly, a victim of kidnapping and extreme brainwashing. She couldn't get away from it. She was just a little girl without parents by her side. No guidance, no protection, and worst, no love. Oh, how much she missed her family. If only she knew the way home. She would have already run away.

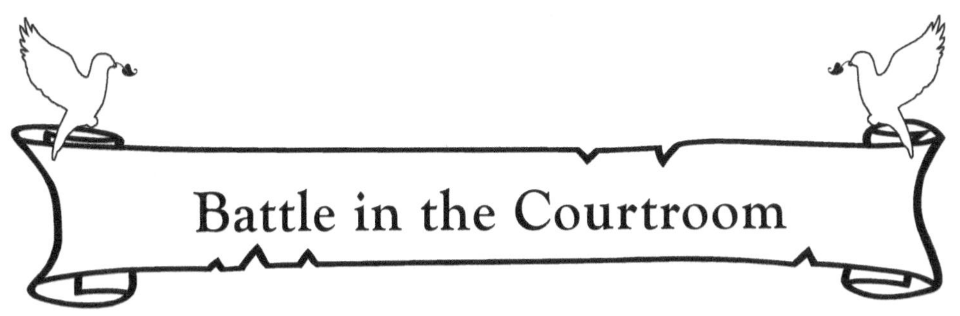

Battle in the Courtroom

*The fight between good and evil is real. Our strong faith in
God will pull us through, one way or another. His help may
not be immediate, but, eventually, you'll be surprised. When
it comes, righteousness wins, and you'll be justified.*

—Ferdinand A. Perez

Shez's new school was a break for her lonely spirit. This was the
atmosphere where she felt love and brief happiness. There was
an abundance of great camaraderie and laughter through learning in
the classroom and playing with friends and classmates. They were
all nice and sweet. Shez hardly had time to think about old friends
from the old neighborhood, but she always thought of kind Jazmine.
She was like a sister. Every after school, she hated the idea of going
back to Mary's house. It was a cold and a lonely residence. She felt a
negative influence in that place. She felt wickedness and evil reigned
in that house. Discomfort and nervousness wrapped her entire being
every time. She wished she was always in school for the most part of
the day. But, eventually, she ignored these ambiguities she felt deep
inside. Shez prayed all the time. She asked for more strength and for-
bearance as she battled her way through her very painful life journey.
We must remember that she was only a little girl. She was only nine.

A few weeks passed. Shez was, once again, summoned to the
lawyer's office. She feared the lawyer's presence. She didn't like him
at all. She was interrogated repeatedly with the same questions, and
she responded with coached, memorized answers as expected. These
questions stuck into her brain like glue that she could no longer dis-
tinguish the truth from lies. It seemed like every word she uttered

was properly documented. It made her more uncomfortable and awkward. But she had no choice. She either testify for them or get beaten up painfully. She was subjected to a very traumatic situation where she was forcefully portrayed to be her father's worst enemy. Her Auntie Mary continuously fed her with negative information about her father. Mary wanted her to seriously loathe her father. And to Mary's delight, her hard work paid off.

Slowly, yet surely, Shez found herself despising her father and brothers. She didn't even want to hear their names mentioned in any manner, shape, or form. She became the worst daughter ever. She was totally brainwashed by Mary. And Mary enjoyed the successful plot to destroy Shez's father through his little princess. Shez sounded very credible during the lawyer's interrogation to the delight of her relatives. She practiced her lines every day to ensure flawless declaration against her father. At long last, Mary felt very prepared and ready to take Shez's father to court with a charge of *homicide*. Shez was completely brainwashed, but at the end of the day, her thoughts remained with her father and brothers. She missed them terribly, but she couldn't express her feelings. She suffered in silence. She shed tears when she was alone and isolated from them.

Shez's maternal relatives finally filed a case against her father. The lawyer immediately started the process. Shez, clueless as she was, had no idea what was happening. She was completely in oblivion, predicated by obscurity and darkness. She abhorred her father and brothers so much, obeyed her Auntie Mary without question, and did everything she could to please her. She likewise changed her image in school, nevertheless, resumed having fun with her new friends. She identified herself as the new Shez—carefree, easygoing, a city girl with a new family. She led her class as expected. Her new friends adored her. And she appeared to be contented and comfortable in school. It was the opposite when she was at the residence of Mary. She was reserved, quiet, isolated, aloof, and lonely. It was like living two separate lives. She was gregarious at school and sad and fearful inside the torture house. Her movements were watched at home.

She couldn't complain or express her mind. She had no opinion on any matter, and she worked more than an ordinary housemaid did.

She was not allowed to sleep at night until all her chores were done. That was how she was treated in her Auntie Mary's house. Of course, her cousin, Lizette, was the princess. Untouchable. Most loved. Most feared. And Shez? She couldn't even talk to Lizette. Lizette had her own crowd, and Shez was not permitted to mingle with any of them.

Shez lived miserably in a fishbowl. For every mistake, she was punished accordingly. Her departed mother's mother (her grandmother) hated her like a leper.

Her grandmother would tell her often, "You're a child of a criminal. You will grow up just like your father."

This sorrowfully made Shez's face grimace horribly. Her father was already branded as such without trial. She locked herself in her bedroom and wept every time her grandmother verbally and physically abused her. Her old grandmother was a wicked witch in disguise. She was abusive and spiteful. She was filled with hatred and loathing toward Shez for no valid reason at all. She enjoyed watching Shez cry and suffer. There was not a day spent without being whipped by her grandmother. Shez lived in fear and agony. It was a painful and melancholic life, a life that was unbearable for a little girl. She was never treated kindly by them. They pretended to show her kindness on vested interest. She did not deserve to be regarded this way. So inhumane. So wicked. She lived a nightmare that she couldn't wake up from. All she could do was cry and pray. She knew that her heavenly Father was there with her, and *he* would never forsake a nine-year-old innocent girl.

The scheduled week came when Shez and relatives traveled to her old city for the much-awaited trial. Mary coached her almost every night on what to say during interrogation. She was prepared and trained to be the star witness against her father. Mary reviewed her testimony several times a day. Once again, the brainwashing was consistently instituted.

Mary told her, "Your father is nothing but a criminal. A murderer. He deserves to rot and die behind bars. Better still, he earned the right to die on the electric chair."

Shez nodded in agreement to every word Mary told her. She was more than terrified, especially when her grandmother snapped with "I'm going to whip you to death if we lose the case."

What a catastrophe! She had an evil grandmother. Horrible. Dreadful. Poor Shez.

The dreadful day came. Mary dressed Shez up expensively, like a rich girl with all the accessories. She looked pampered and well taken care of. It was a show. Mary loved to show people how rich they were and how Shez was a very lucky girl. Shez, on the other hand, was on the brink of collapse. She never felt so nervous and scared before. Puppet Shez. She would do anything to please Mary. She was completely programmed. Indoctrinated. There were no words left to describe Shez's pathetic situation, and her family had no idea. Her siblings hated her for betraying them. Her father was extremely disappointed with her. And they had no clue as to what situation Shez was dealing with. They simply had no idea how Shez survived under Mary's care.

Shez and relatives came into the courtroom, earlier than the accused. She saw her father walked in with the saddest face ever. Somber and muted with two guards on each side. He looked pale and gaunt. Head bowed and did not look toward Shez's way. He looked isolated and detached. Shez's siblings were behind him. JoJo, the oldest brother, threw a quick glance toward Shez with a gloomy face. The siblings did not appear excited to see her at that point. They despised her. So sad. The family was totally broken and fragmented. Shez was no longer deemed as one of them. She was an outcast. She was considered as the female version of Judas Iscariot. She betrayed her own. They didn't want her anymore. She was considered dead as far as they were concerned. The once-upon-a-time happy family was shattered and hopeless. It then became a case of Shez versus her own family.

The session had begun. Lawyers from the two sides started battling and arguing. Shez could hardly grasp the conversation completely, but she didn't care. She sat beside Mary in silence. Her whole body shook in fear, and her sweet prayers were uttered unceasingly that only God could hear. She was confused on what to do. Torn between two different families. Each had high expectations from

Shez. It was like hitting a huge brick wall on both sides, and there was no way out to escape. She was trapped. Cornered. Stuck. She felt like she was the one on trial. She felt like all the blame was upon her. Was she intended to be a victim all the time? *God only knows.*

Second day of the battle in the courtroom came. This time, Shez was called by her relatives' lawyer onto the witness stand. She trembled as she approached the stand cautiously yet radiated confidence. With a serious look, she raised her right hand as instructed to speak the truth and nothing but the truth. She flinched a bit. She bit her lips. She turned pale. She knew she would be telling lies in front of the judge (there were no juries since their justice system was different in that country), her father and siblings, her relatives, the entire audience, and God. She sat on the witness stand quietly responding only to what was questioned from her. The lawyer asked Shez to narrate the tragedy the way it unfolded before her eyes. And, yes, the lies began. The lies echoed throughout the courtroom like lightning. Silence wrapped the room jampacked with nosy people. Because Shez was just a nine-year-old little girl, her story sounded so plausible. Legit. Authentic. Genuine. They had no idea how Shez's story came about. All were coerced. Practiced. Wickedly fabricated. False. Deceit. She kept her testimony intact and flawless. Such a smart girl. A vicious, smart girl. Her Auntie Mary must have been very proud of her. She saw her father sob from the right corner of her eye as she threw a quick glance upon him.

"How could she?" JoJo, the oldest sibling mutedly whispered to himself.

"Where did she get the manufactured story?"

"She wasn't even present when it occurred."

"Such a big liar," snapped the other sibling.

For Shez, it was a terrible mistake. She wanted to tell everyone that she lied, but she was frozen. She was petrified. Incapacitated. There was no more turning back. Her fate was sealed. She was officially the enemy number one of her family. The session was called off through the stern voice of the judge as he raised the gavel and exited the scene. Chaos ensued as everyone got off their seats. Shez, with her relatives, likewise departed the courthouse full of hope and excitement. They all told Shez that she did an excellent job during the investigation. Silence took over Shez. No words. No comments.

The following day, everyone involved came back to the courtroom. This time, the defendant's team was on the floor. The siblings were called to testify. One by one, they raised their right hand and swore to tell the truth and nothing but the truth. JoJo, the oldest, was called first. He testified what exactly happened since Shez was aware that her oldest brother was present during the tragedy. Shez, for the first time, heard JoJo's testimony. She finally learned the truth. The real thing. She concluded that everything was an accident. Her father did not shoot her mother. The relatives concocted the whole story with their own wild version. They fabricated the whole story that brainwashed the little girl to begin with. She was made to believe that her father shot her mother to death. They were wrong. Dead wrong. Shez was happy to know what really happened during that fatal day. She was delighted to know that her father was an innocent man after all. And she was a big liar in the real sense of the word. She could not forgive herself for what she did to her family, especially to her father.

She wanted to ask forgiveness right there but was too fearful to do so. Her Auntie Mary would surely beat her up with a leather belt or with a piece of wood. She was terrified. All she did at that very moment was cry in silence. She repented in silence and felt remorseful on what she did to her family.

The homicide case came into a conclusion after a week of testimony after testimony. Shez's departed mother's lover was nowhere to be seen. It was such an emotional trauma on her part. And, for sure, her siblings felt the same way. She avoided eye contact with her siblings. More so with her father. She was too humiliated and embarrassed. She felt defeated and useless. She was misled by Mary. Mary used her to break the family apart and put all the blame on her father. To sum up: Shez's departed mother started having an affair first, and disastrous consequences fell upon them. Evil came in different shapes and forms. The family allowed evil to walk through them that ultimately tore them apart. Hence, a fragmented family they became.

The verdict came back after one week. The charge was recalibrated into accidental death, and Shez's father was found not guilty.

It was a big victory for the defendant. Shez's father was finally set free. Shez didn't understand the verdict at first (she was only nine, remember?) but was glad that Mary's wish of a lifetime prison sentence didn't come into fruition. Mary was livid. She spent so much money to put Shez's father behind bars for good but failed. Shez was thankful for the outcome. No huge damage done toward her father. The only thing that saddened her most was her separation from the family she loved the most. Her siblings didn't want her. They avoided her at all costs. She was not only motherless, but she also lost her entire family. Was she happy and contented living with her maternal relatives? Or was she completely broken and unhappy? What happened to Shez under Mary's roof after these awful events? We will surely know as we turn to more chapters of this book.

She hid all the pain and suffering behind a facade. Behind her Monalisa smile was a world of turmoil and misery. You thought you knew her well, but you really had no idea. Her innocent little life was full of secrets and mystery. "Poor Shez!"

—*Susie A. Perez*

Shez and her relatives packed their stuff up and headed to their city after attending a week of courtroom drama. It was a day of reckoning on her part. She didn't know that it would take at least ten years to be reunited with her oldest brother, JoJo, and an additional five years to be back in her old hometown and be reunited with her father—fifteen long, agonizing years to see her father again. She didn't know that she would never see Jazmine and her other good friends again. And she didn't know that she was on her way to a very sad, miserable, depressing life ahead of her. Oh, Shez! If only you knew! If only you knew! You would not hesitate to go back to your father's care, to go home to your own siblings and feel the love that you have deeply longed for.

Shez began to live a new life that was full of woes and misery under Mary's wings after the traumatic courtroom drama. Mary imposed a rule that isolated Shez from her father and siblings. She had no way to communicate with her family at any given time. She missed her immediate family so much, yet she was not permitted to express it. She cried by herself secretly since there was no support whatsoever from her relatives. She was monitored and heavily watched on everything she did. Mary continued to send her to school and the same time made Shez labor hard at home. She was given various chores that were quite severe and heavy for a nine-year-old girl. She worked with the rest of the housemaids in the house. She ate and slept with them. She was cast out of Lizette's bedroom (they used to be roommates) and shared sleeping quarters with the maids.

On the outside, she didn't look sore at all. She tried to put on a happy face. She was dying deep inside her. Brokenhearted and emotionally beaten. She had nowhere to run. Her other aunties and uncles were all intimidated by Mary. They were powerless to help Shez. She was torn between two tough walls, and there was no way out. Eventually, she felt that she deserved all the punishments for what she did to her father and brothers. She resignedly accepted her misfortunes with a fragmented heart and tried her best to move on. She worked so hard, maintained her good grades in school, and suffered all the beatings she got daily. There was never a day that she was not beaten by her grandmother. Shez was painfully abused physically, verbally, and emotionally. She cried herself to sleep almost every night. Her transient happy moments were spent in school with friends and classmates who were clueless about her house situation. Oh, if she could only spend 24-7 at school, she would be very grateful.

Amazingly, she never lost hope, though. She knew that God was watching her very carefully. She accepted her retribution for what she did, and she was fine with it. Her small, fragile body got used to the beatings and felt numb about the negative occurrences around her. Shez was hardened physically and emotionally. She became tough. She fought back to the beatings she got by mockingly tolerating the pain. She no longer cried or felt sorry for herself. She told herself that she was not scared anymore. She expressed the idea of killing herself to her friends at school, but no one paid attention to her. The everyday beatings she got from her grandmother became a routine for her. She accepted the painful lashes with silence and detachment. She intentionally disconnected herself from her physical body to tolerate the whippings. She silently became a rebel of her own. There were days that she wouldn't eat or talk. She angrily talked back to anyone, even to her Auntie Mary, whenever she was scolded.

She didn't care when Mary slapped her face several times for talking back. Shez most likely got tired of playing a victim. She refused to be one. They could whip her body all they want, but she just got increasingly stubborn and tenacious. She changed for the worst. She stole money from them, occasionally (since Mary stopped giving her school allowance), whenever she had things to purchase for school projects. She surprisingly survived in the environment she was in. The more the relatives, especially Mary and her grandmother, treated her like trash, the stronger she became. Shez was inappropriately placed in a grim situation. No parents, no siblings, no one. She became her own little world with packs of wolves around, ready to devour a little child. She became her own defender. She was only nine but quickly matured in thinking and reasoning.

Despite the catastrophes, she consistently prayed for guidance, protection, and forgiveness to the Lord. She talked to God daily and continued loving her father and siblings. She looked forward to seeing them once again. As to when? She had no idea.

Shez, otherwise, was doing well in school. She maintained her topnotcher position in all of her classes and was well-liked by teachers and classmates. Sporadically, she thought of her best friend, Jazmine, and her other previous classmates. She would often daydream and reminisce the happy moments she unfortunately left behind. Was she sorry for leaving her family behind? Absolutely! Was she remorseful on what she did to her father? Definitely! If she could only turn the time back, she would in a second. She understood time would keep ticking. There was no turning back. Repentance always came at the last moment in one's life. And she was no exception.

Shez completed her fourth grade in the new school satisfactorily. She was awarded a gold medal as the class valedictorian. She was so pleased with it. She thought of her loving father and brothers almost all the time. She was positive that they would be happy for her. Mary and the rest didn't acknowledge her success, but who cared? Shez shared her achievement with friends and classmates. She turned ten and was ready to tackle middle school. There was no celebration that took place on her tenth birthday. Instead, she was reprimanded to work in the garden under the scorching heat of the sun. Nevertheless, Mr. Wind was never away. The soft, cool breeze around Shez's workplace made it tolerable for hard labor. She continued her usual heavy routine chores at home and fun activities in school.

On the contrary, she was excited as her learning ladder got higher and her education perspective got broader. She was filled with high ambitions and impossible dreams. She wanted to become a lawyer someday as her horizon had widened and her priorities had changed. She was more mature yet happy-go-lucky at school. Nothing could stop her dreams. She was determined to pursue what she wanted in life, regardless.

One sunny and quiet Saturday, Shez saw an opportunity to escape. Not one of her relatives was at home. The housemaids were busy with chores, and she was left by herself, tending the garden. She cautiously opened the house gate and, without hesitation, ran as fast as she could. She was running for her freedom. She was running for her life. She didn't turn back as she aimed to return to her old community where her father and siblings lived. She just kept on running. Unfortunately, she didn't know where the bus terminal was located, and she was penniless. All she did was run away from them. She prayed and hoped that she would meet a good Samaritan who could come to her rescue as drops of sweat dripped down unceasingly on her sweet face. She was unrelentingly relentless. She ran without direction. She was unstoppable.

After hours of running, she heard a loud whistle. When Shez turned around, she saw a police officer approach her. Her whole world turned upside down. She was inadvertently caught. Her face turned white as a bond paper, and she lamentingly cried. The officer took her hand kindly. He comforted her. He told her that her Auntie Mary reported her a runaway and that she needed to go back to her relatives. What can a little girl do at that moment? Nothing! She nodded her head as a sign of defeat and total submission. Shez knew that she would be beaten till she dropped dead. She prepared herself physically and emotionally. She decided to cease crying and get prepared for whatever punishment she would get. Mary, the monster, and the rest of the wicked clan met her with angry faces.

"You're disgusting," were the first words she heard from Mary. "You're just like your father! Good for nothing. Ungrateful pig. You're an embarrassment to the family!" Mary added in a condescending manner.

"Worthless," Lizette remarked with a disdainful look at Shez's face.

She was treated inhumanely. She was slapped, beaten, abused, and assaulted. She was a perfect picture of an abused, helpless child that was unloved by the people she trusted before. She was totally defenseless. Utterly orphaned. Unloved. Neglected. Abandoned. She was not offered any food or water to drink that fateful day. They denied her basic sustenance. The only comfort she got was from her little dog named Frisky. Frisky stayed by her side the entire night. The atrocities that her relatives committed against her could be grounds for a child abuse case if it happened at the present time. Unluckily for Shez, there was no such thing as child abuse during that time. This little girl suffered so much under Mary's care. She gave her full trust to them during her vulnerable times nonetheless. She made a huge mistake. She was completely betrayed. She had not imagined herself to belong to such a dysfunctional family. Living under Mary's roof was more than a torture. It was burning her alive. And there was no way to escape. There was zero relief in plain sight.

Right after the incident, Mary decided to lock Shez up in a room for a while as the wicked grandmother watched her like a hawk with a whip in her hand. It was so inhumane. How could they do this to a child? Instead of showing her love and acceptance, they showered her with cruelty unbefitting to a child whose only yearning was to love and be loved. How could you consistently abuse a little girl who had been helpless and vulnerable since she was kidnapped? They fed her with a paper plate inside that room where she was treated like a prisoner. Shez could hardly breathe freely as she watched her grandmother's evil eyes look at her fiercely. She could only pray harder to have this ordeal vanish. At her age, the traumatic experiences that had occurred in her life intensified like no other. Until how much longer could this little girl tackle and tolerate these inevitable storms? Until when? Only God knew.

The abuse continued every day. As expected, Shez got used to the scolding and beatings. Those harsh words and painful lashes became a normal way of life for her. She was handled horribly. The maids were treated far better off. There were no words to describe her bitter life during those times. Days became weeks. Weeks became months. Months became years, yet Shez's living condition had remained the same. She was abused, given the harshest tasks to perform, not fed properly, not even dressed properly. She was already twelve years old at this point, but her body build looked like ten, and she appeared malnourished, emaciated, and pale. She got those hand-me-down clothes from Lizette, and her heart sweetly swelled with gratitude. Her neighbors occasionally fed her with no questions asked. For the most part, Shez avoided their next-door-neighbors. She didn't want to start any gossip or innuendos around the neighborhood. She usually kept to herself and remained totally isolated.

Shez finally graduated from middle school as the valedictorian. There was no celebration in her Auntie Mary's residence. She was quietly delighted and thankful to her heavenly Father. Her outlook in life was full of hope and aspiration as she looked forward to high school. She was a budding teenager at that time and had a zest for what lay ahead. She gratefully commemorated a milestone to herself and by herself.

She thought, *If only my family was here. They would surely be proud of me.*

She delivered her valedictory address enthusiastically and passionately. She meant everything she said.

"Success is sweeter when shared with people you love," she said as tears started rolling down her cheeks.

Her vibrant speech as a child commended with a standing ovation from the crowd. Her relatives were not in attendance, but she didn't care at all. It was an emotional moment. Shez, being alone, parentless, no siblings, no moral support, nothing at all and, yet, there she proudly stood in front of a cheering crowd who listened and agreed to her talk and most especially adored her from afar. As for me, being a friend that she completely trusted, I conclude, without reservation, that Shez is truly a diamond in the rough.

High school is an essential stage of someone's life. It is a bridge between childhood and adulthood where one can develop lasting friendships and worst enemies. And, more importantly, it is the beginning period of finding your true self and your real purpose in life.

—*Susie A. Perez*

Shez continued her aspiration to stay in school, no matter what. She didn't care about the hard work given to her by Mary. Shez did everything she asked to please all of them. She had no school allowance, and to survive the ordeal, she would bring a meager rice and dried fish wrapped in banana leaves for lunch. She walked a few kilometers to school daily and would likewise hike home. It was quite an effort, but she did what she had to do. She maintained her academic status in high school, despite multiple competitions among classmates. The only barrier was the extracurricular activities. Mary did not finance any projects she had; thus, she was always late in project submission. Mary did not fulfill all the promises she made to the judge during the habeas corpus hearing. She promised to provide everything for the little girl, hence the judge awarded her the custody. Mary intentionally forgot what she swore in the courtroom. She heartlessly abused the little girl. She maliciously used her for hard labor. She maltreated her. She neglected her.

Shez didn't receive the mother's love she longed for from Mary. She was terribly betrayed. She had issues trusting other people, let alone her own relatives because of the traumatic experiences she was in. She was just a piece of garbage in Mary's house. She was not fed well. She was hungry all the time. Confusion, dizziness, and fainting spells were a few signs that were exhibited by Shez in school. She was embarrassed and humiliated every time these things happened. Despite all these, Shez persevered and endured all the difficulties, just to be in school. Her love for learning never faded, notwithstanding the obstacles she faced daily. *"Persistence is the key to success"* was her mantra, and she intended to follow it, whatever the cost maybe.

It was during her junior year in high school when an intelligent, shy classmate caught her eyes. He was so good-looking yet timid. Shez supposed it was reciprocal since she sometimes caught the boy's glimpses toward her way. This boy gave her inspiration to study harder and live happier despite the worsened conditions at home. She thought of him, especially in times of sadness and despair, in times of sorrow and grief. The boy's bashful smiles were like her pep medication daily. She admired him from a distance. She wished to become his friend. He seemed to be so near yet so far.

"Does he know I have a huge crush on him?" Shez asked her good friend and classmate, Claire.

"Most likely," Claire responded. "He looks delighted every time he sees you," Claire continued.

Claire's comments made Shez's heart beat even faster. She wished to know more about him but was too embarrassed due to her heartbreaking situation.

"Who would love someone like me? I'm a nobody, a worthless human being who has nothing in life but big dreams and ambitions and nothing else. I'm poorer than the mouse that lives in that little hole in the kitchen," Shez said to herself and cried.

For the first time in Shez's brittle life, she liked or perchance loved someone from the opposite sex, aside from her family. Shez was indeed growing up physically and emotionally.

Shez had the boy's name written all over her school notes. She even mentioned his name in her diary. She was careful not to tell anyone at home, especially her Auntie Mary or cousin Lizette. She feared they might beat her up even more. We must remember that Shez got beat up, regardless of reasons, daily. She was extra vigilant of not divulging sweet secrets to anyone in the house. It might have been difficult for her to grow up without parents. She needed someone to confide her puppy loves, high school crushes, and any teenage escapades, but there was no one that would listen to her. Her friend, Claire, was a great listener and the only one that listened to her, but Shez needed a parent with an unconditional love to understand and guide her during this period. Teenage life could be unbridled when not properly handled.

Adolescence is a difficult stage, and we all passed it once in our lifetime. Proper guidance and care are needed to raise a child into a full bloom, responsible, kind, and caring adult. There are no magic rules that parents utilize in raising children appropriately into adulthood, but with the unconditional love offered, a child passes the delicate stage successfully and confidently. The child may not be perfect but will be able to confidently thrive in his/her own imperfections and flaws. Acceptance, tolerance, and motivation follow when the child is justly supervised. Shez passed this stage by herself. No proper guidance at all. Her teachers in school could care less about her. However, the teachers did a great job on guiding her academically. Mary and other relatives didn't care about Shez either. It was up to her on how she would manage her life and future. She was all she got. No more. No less.

High school days came and went, and, finally, Shez was a senior in high school. Her hope of finishing secondary education was almost accomplished. Excitement was in the air now that she was a candidate for graduation. She was ecstatic and thrilled. She could not believe that she made it this far. The admiration she developed toward the shy, intelligent boy in her class had remained intact. She wished the boy knew her feelings. She dreamed of great beautiful things about him. She truly loved and adored the boy who seemed to have reciprocated the feelings and, yet, was aloof to the idea of becoming high school sweethearts. He appeared to be focused on his studies, and he indeed excelled academically. Shez and Claire remained good friends and helped each other in school projects and homework.

The home front situation lingered and believed to be getting worse and unlivable. Shez was consistently abused in all aspects, yet the little girl who grew up to be a strong-willed, determined, teenager had lived it all. She may not have the best clothes to wear or the most money to spend, yet she was rich in aspiration and ambition. She didn't allow her miserable life under Mary's roof ruin her journey to success. Shez was indeed a teenager on a mission. On the other hand, she never lost faith that, one day, she would reunite with her father and siblings again. She never stopped thinking of them, and nights were still lonely without them by her side.

It was in the middle of Shez's senior year when she heard awful news about her father. A big-mouthed, little birdie told Mary that Shez's father had remarried some five years ago. Shez was stunned! *Five years ago? And nobody knew? Why?* she wondered.

"My father must have totally forgotten me," she whimpered. She then wondered what happened to her siblings. *"They must be all grown-up at this time,"* she quipped.

As to what had transpired among them, Shez desperately wanted to know.

Mary came with more unwelcomed news. "JoJo, your oldest brother, is in the military while your other brothers are attending college, north of the country."

Shez had paradoxical feelings about it. She realized that her family had disbanded and parted. Her father had a new family (wife and children), JoJo was married and in the military, the rest of her brothers were living with other people in a faraway city to finish college. And she was with Mary, living desolately under the most horrible condition. Her nightmare prophetically continued. Things had not gone better; in fact, everything had turned worse than she thought. She couldn't return to her father, she didn't know where her brothers were, and she wasn't sure if college was in her future. Would she remain a housemaid under Mary's roof? Would she attend college? These questions were in her mind most of the time. She was desperate. She didn't know where to turn to.

Shez confided her issues to Claire who was all ears and sympathetic to her. Claire invited her to live with her family, but Shez declined. Claire belonged to a poor family as well, with an alcoholic, jobless father. Claire's mother did odd jobs to sustain the family of nine. Shez didn't see herself living with them. It would be a burden on the part of Claire's family. Both shared laughter and tears all throughout high school and treated each other like sisters. Both were broken with depressing situations, while trying their best to be normal teenagers. Life had treated these two girls unfairly. But whatever the consequences were at that time, they triumphantly conquered them with flying colors.

High school graduation came. Shez was as excited as could be. She informed her Auntie Mary and the rest of the relatives about the commencement day, but no one appeared thrilled. She was completely ignored and unappreciated. This behavior didn't bother Shez at all. She got used to being treated like she didn't exist. She planned on attending the ceremony and looked forward to speaking with her high school crush at that event. The shy boy that Shez admired never talked to her after all those years. They just exchanged glances and smiled at each other, and that was all.

"He better talk to me at our graduation ceremony," snapped Shez to Claire. "After all, that will be our last day together with all our classmates."

"Fingers crossed." Claire happily agreed.

Graduation songs were practiced daily. Speeches were rehearsed, and, unluckily, Shez didn't bag the valedictorian spot due to many circumstances. The extracurricular activities threw her out of the honor roll because of financial difficulties. She had no money to buy projects, to participate in leadership programs, to contribute to any committees. She could hardly afford the tuition fees and other required fees. Mary gave her a hard time with everything that pertained to financial contributions and payments in school. No allowance, no support at all. She begged and pleaded for everything to finish high school. She tirelessly worked hard at home to survive, without complaints whatsoever. Shez did well academically, but to be in the honor roll, the student needed to excel in every department. And she was aware of the requirements, no regrets at all, and was even grateful that she would finally graduate from high school. It was an achievement that she was proud of, and she was thankful for the blessings from God.

Graduation ceremony came. Every graduate looked dazzling and joyful. The graduates' families were in attendance. Laughter echoed the gymnasium. The band was playing loudly. Graduates beamed with pride. Their caps and gowns were impressive. The choir was in full swing as the graduates marched toward their seats. Suddenly, the noise became solemn and poignant. The choir's song complemented Shez's broken heart as tears came rolling down her cheeks, when the words of the song were sung.

Speeches were spoken, distinguished awards were given to deserving students and, finally, names were called up the stage to get the most-sought high school diploma. Audience thundered with their hands vigorously applauding as the graduates' names were called one by one. And the entire sixty graduates finally back to their seats, and with a quick signal, threw their caps in the air, audience celebrated, and the band played "Congratulations" gleefully. The graduates then rendered the traditional "alma mater hymn" for all to hear. And that was that. Shez didn't have the opportunity to talk to her big-time crush or puppy love. He was gone with his family while Shez was left by herself, in a cheering crowd. Claire was taken by her family for celebration, and Shez was simply by herself. No family. No relatives. No one came and shared her milestone, her accomplishment that she labored so hard to achieve. Suddenly, the place was quiet and dead silent. Everyone had gone away. There was no one there but the school janitor and the principal who noted her presence.

"Why are you still here?" asked the principal. "Are you waiting for your family to come pick you up?"

Shez nodded as she wiped her tears away. "Ah, yes, sir. They should be here any minute now." She hurriedly exited the gym and soulfully walked away from her beloved high school ground. The high school campus was her only source of joy during those four lamenting years of misery and despair. This was the place where her heart beat lovingly as her crush walked past her. This was the place where she could just be herself. Happy and carefree, together with her best friend, Claire. Now this campus became one of her joyous memories that she treasured most dearly in her lifetime. Mournfully, Shez slowly trod bound for the house that she hated to live in. The house of torture where Mary and the rest were waiting for her impatiently and callously.

SUMMER SURPRISE

*To reunite and reminisce with families and friends that you have
not seen for a long time is one of the best opportunities you can
have in your lifetime. It is a chance to share memories, good or
bad, and will once more bring back the good old, loving feelings.*

—*Porferio R. Angus, Jr.*

High school days were gone, and the summer season was staring at Shez's face intensely and warmly. She loved the hot and sunny weather where flowers bloomed, butterflies and bees and even dragonflies were abundant, and Mr. Wind was a constant presence anywhere she went. She recalled her happy days with her old friends from the old neighborhood where they happily spent most of their time playing in the singing brook and carelessly collected froggies along the way. Those carefree, magical moments were constantly in her mind, regardless of what she was doing. She thought of her dear best friend, Jasmine, and her other good friends, nonetheless. And, most of all, her happy family that was broken and fragmented by unexpected tragedy. The mystical moon, the amazing constellation up in the sky, and the fireflies' light at night made her quiver as she once again thought of her childhood days. Ah, the warm breeze of summer. Memories, pleasant and bad, came rolling into Shez's mind like a piece of notepad that was filled with dust and dirt and subsequently left on the shelf. She couldn't help but smile tenderly on those lovely moments she left behind but never to be forgotten. She may not be able to bring back her happy childhood, but those tender loving remembrances lingered with her for life.

As usual, Shez worked so hard when she was home. Hard labor was her full-time job every summer under Mary's roof. She was Lizette's private help daily, plus other hard works in the house. She was treated as one of their maids at any given time. She did her daily chores with a happy yet melancholic heart. She was always nostalgic of her family and old friends. She missed her departed mother as well. Yet she worked with a song in her heart to pass the time quickly and to lighten up the load. Shez was fond of humming love songs all day long while working, and sometimes, her grandmother beat her up, just because of that. Obviously, her grandmother hated songs and happy things. She was so inhumane. Sadistic and vicious.

One evening after dinner, Shez was doing dishes when she was summoned by her Auntie Mary. "Come over to the living room, quick," demanded Mary.

Shez jumped from the kitchen and hurriedly walked toward the living room. To her amazement, she saw JoJo, her oldest brother, happily standing right in front of her. She was speechless. She could not believe it. She was flabbergasted. She stood frozen in front of her brother, then she bawled. She wept bitterly, and JoJo sobbed with her. They embraced. After almost ten years, here she was, hugging her long-lost brother. It was a very heartbreaking scene. A memorable meeting. Both felt awkward at first, but after the dramatic initial meeting, they felt comfortable with each other once again. It was like the good old times. *Blood indeed is thicker than water.* JoJo looked older. He appeared exhausted yet glad to see his baby sister. Mary invited JoJo for dinner and, afterward, allowed Shez to be with her brother, instead of doing chores. Shez and JoJo spent the precious moment catching up.

"How's Papa?" asked Shez.

"He's been married for many years now," responded JoJo.

Shez was silent. JoJo interrupted her deep thoughts. "He missed you, you know. There was not a day he spent without thinking of you. He would quietly cry every time your name came up in conversations," JoJo continued with tears in his eyes.

JoJo further exposed how he and the other siblings were maltreated by the stepmother, how their father's second wife made up crazy stories to gain their father's sympathy against them, how she pretended to be the real victim because of them. Unfortunately, their father always sided with his new wife, every time an argument occurred. This was one of the many reasons why JoJo and the other siblings decided to part ways with their father, especially when the couple started having children of their own. Powerful yet painful words from JoJo's revelation regarding their family. But Shez remained mum. Once again, she felt shattered. Her heart, once again, was broken. She felt her entire body and soul were subjected to oblivion, where misery and despair dwell. Oh, how she wished her family would unite and be together again. But how? Her father obviously had his own family, leaving her and her siblings out of the equation.

"Nothing will be the same after all these years," cried Shez.

Everything was torn to pieces. Every heart was broken, leaving them all fragmented into tiny bits of tears that were blown away into nothingness and void. Her hope that was built deep within her soul crushed like a poor tiny spider who tried her best to web her beautiful home but was washed away by a mere splash of water from the unforgiving rain. Shez lost it. She sobbed. She was miserable.

JoJo comforted her. "It's okay. Life is not always perfect. You'll get used to having a stepmother and half siblings, just like I did," he stated.

"My mother is irreplaceable," snapped Shez. "And I don't need a stepmother in my own little abandoned world," she added.

Shez was grief-stricken. She was delighted to see JoJo but was devastated with the news he brought with him. However, their conversation went on for hours. Shez confided in JoJo on how she was treated under Mary's roof, on her college plans and her ambition in life. She did seek JoJo's assistance in terms of finances for college, just in case she needed it, and JoJo, without hesitation, promised to help her. They both recollected the happy moments of their childhood in the old neighborhood where their father resided with his new family. It was so emotional. There were no arguments, just pure brother-sister love as they happily took advantage of the opportunity that was given to them. Both expressed gratitude of finally seeing each other, and their Auntie Mary offered JoJo a space to spend the night, but he refused. He reasoned the need to report back to the camp where he was assigned, lest he'd be marked as AWOL.

The moment came when JoJo had to leave. Sad goodbyes were quietly uttered with gloomy faces. JoJo reassured his little sister that he'd be back but couldn't predict the exact time. He was assigned anywhere and everywhere as military personnel; thus, his destination changed without proper notice. Shez completely understood her brother's situation. She didn't object or argue. Their journeys were different, and their priorities had changed. It wasn't the same when they were children living under one roof with the same set of parents. The basic settings had changed. Both were nostalgic and sad as they parted. Tender hugs were exchanged, and then, JoJo was out of sight. It was such an emotionally draining farewell.

Shez remained standing by the gate as she watched her oldest brother walked away until she could no longer see him. She chased him as much as she could as she continuously waved her hand. Tears were seen from her cheeks, eyes swollen, and silent sobs heard as she whispered mutedly her sad goodbye.

"*Bye, my dear brother*"—she breathed—"*Until we meet again. God bless and keep you safe always.*"

And that was that. JoJo slowly vanished from her view. Reality checked in right after the moving parting scene. Shez was immediately summoned by Mary to resume her chores. Of course, no one could escape Mary's wrath and iron fist. Shez needed to work to eat. To live. She tidied the kitchen, fed the animals, did the dishes, cleaned the stove, swept, and mopped the floors before she was allowed to rest and sleep. Most of the time, the household tasks took her up to midnight to finally get done. She worked without any complaints. She was focused and intended to get things done before midnight. Her dog, Frisky, kept her company throughout the ordeal. Quietly yet steadily, she cleaned the floor, mopped it with a double stroke style that somehow made her do some dance moves like a fairy lost in the wonderland. She did it until the floors shone like an enchanted place found in fairyland. Shez tried her best to have fun in everything she did in the house of torture.

A few weeks after the sweet reunion with her oldest brother, JoJo, Shez got ill. She had an elevated temperature, chills, shakes, and was throwing up violently. At first, no one paid attention to her. They made her work, regardless of her unknown illness. She hesitantly obeyed their orders until she noticed rashes all over her body that were itchy, fluid-filled blisters. They first appeared in her chest, back, and face and quickly spread over the entire body—including inside her mouth that made it impossible to eat—her eyelids, ears, armpits, and genitals. Her fever went sky-high and made Shez delusional and claustrophobic. Mary, once again, isolated Shez until the symptoms were gone and the fever subsided. It took Shez around four weeks or so to fully recover from the awful disease called chicken pox.

A couple of weeks had passed when Shez found her dog, Frisky, not as active and playful as he used to be. He was merely lying by the side of the residence in silence. Shez approached her beloved dog and found out that Frisky was hardly breathing. Exasperated, Shez called her cousin Ben to help her with Frisky. They carried Frisky toward the kitchen and assessed him. Frisky was breathless and gone. Shez, once again, found herself alone and abandoned. Frisky was the only one who was always at her side in everything she did at home. He was her constant companion. Loyal and devoted, he had this magic to cheer her up, regardless of the situation. He was all she got in the place of torture. Her beloved pet that served as her inspiration daily. Again, she was shattered and broken.

"Why does God take the people I love away from me all the time?" she asked herself as she was grieving for Frisky.

Cousin Ben comforted and assisted her as both dug the ground in the backyard to bury Frisky. They performed a simple ceremony for Frisky as they said their goodbyes to the beloved dog.

That summer was memorable for Shez. She finally met her oldest brother, JoJo, and bonded with him once again and, on the other hand, she lost Frisky, her constant companion during the happy and lonely days. She felt so alone when Frisky died. Once again, the word *isolated* echoed loudly, deep within her aching and grieving heart.

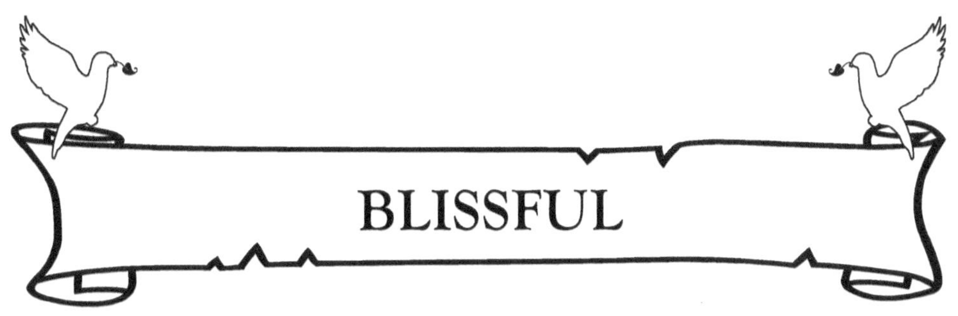

BLISSFUL

*Follow your bliss faithfully, And the kind universe will
wonderfully open the doors and windows wide, for you,
where initially, there are only walls around.*

—*Porferio R. Angus, Jr.*

One Saturday morning, Shez markedly noticed huge, dark, ominous clouds dressed the sky in black, and they appeared full and heavy and ready to burst any minute. Quickly, a powerful thunder rolled up above her, followed by a frightening flash of an overwhelming lightning. And, yes, a copious downpour of silent rain was seen everywhere. A commanding rainstorm just occurred. Strong winds ripped all over the city, causing havoc to trees, houses, and anything that crossed its way. Devastation and mayhem immediately took over the place. The entire city was dark and dreary. It was a terrifying day. The entire community was dripping wet and wild. Right there and then, Shez unintentionally thought of her beloved childhood and fondly recalled her youthful days of running and splashing puddles under the rain, together with Jazmine and others. She tightly closed her eyes, and swiftly, all those happy memories came rushing into her mind and soul. She smiled a bit and sighed. She wished! Just wished something positive would cross her way today, despite the gloomy weather. It was wishful thinking that she would cherish forever.

It was past lunchtime when the weather calmed down a bit. It was still raining but not as aggressive as earlier that day. The sun quietly creeped from behind the clouds and lighted the city with its sharp, yellow rays. The sunshine scattered radiance and warmth that Shez could not ignore. It brightened her gloomy day, so to speak.

"The sun's up," whispered Shez to herself.

She was delighted to feel the sunshine in her face as she opened the maid's quarter's little window to get a glimpse of the destruction left by the compelling rainstorm. She extended her right hand out of the window and felt the tiny drops of the falling rain and breathed Mr. Wind's cold air that accompanied it. It was mesmerizing. Yes, it caused havoc to people, but at the same time, it reminded Shez of God's omnipotence and supremacy.

"To God be the glory," she softly hummed with tears in her eyes and a sweet smile on her lips.

Ding-dong, rang the doorbell. Someone was at the gate. One of the maids got out and opened the gate where a soaked postman stood. He smilingly handed an airmail envelop and hurriedly left. The maid gave the letter to Shez as it was addressed to her. Mary, Lizette, and others, who were at the living room, stopped their conversation as Shez eagerly opened the letter. As she started reading the letter, she went moon-eyed. Stunned. She was staring at the letter in amazement. She was speechless.

"Give me that!" snapped Lizette condescendingly as she snottily grabbed the letter.

She, too, was goggle-eyed. She threw the letter to her mother, Mary, who was quite contrary on what just happened. And then they all learned the whole truth. Shez was accepted into a prestigious university college of law and was awarded a full academic scholarship from tuition, books, room, and board. They could not believe Shez's luck. They were dumbfounded.

"They have got to be kidding!" yelled Mary. "This is surreal." Mary stood up from where she was sitting, went to Shez, and grabbed her hair. "How did you manage applying to some university without my permission?" she angrily snarled. "Are you doing things behind my back to get even with me?" Mary sneered sarcastically. Her eyes went black with anger. She deliberately slapped Shez's face, called her ingrate, and tore the acceptance letter into pieces. Shez's face blushed, and she remained muted.

Shez was alone in the living room as they all left after the heartless episode. She was numbed. She didn't feel the pain or the hurt that was inflicted to her. She stood silently with a stoic face and surprisingly without shedding a single tear.

"I will fight for my right! I will pursue this for my own future and get out of this torture place for my own sanity," she softly yet sternly whispered to herself.

She quickly gathered the pieces of the torn letter, ran to the maid's quarter, and started connecting and taping the pieces for her to completely review the instructions given on how to accept the proposal and enter the university.

After a few days, Shez was able to form the letter into one readable piece. She then penned a short response informing the college of law admission office that she accepted the offer and gave the date of her arrival and would check into St. Bernadette's ladies dorm, which was located at the main university campus. She then wrote a short note to her oldest brother, JoJo, to inform of her whereabouts in approximately one month from that eventful day. She expressed excitement and yet fearful of what was going to transpire in the next four weeks of her young life.

"Am I really university-bound?" she asked herself this question several times a day. *"Will I be able to maintain the grade the university expected from me to achieve and continue my academic scholarship till I graduate?* What if? What if?" she paused and again composed and reassured herself that she could do this.

She was adamant that she could achieve her dream through perseverance, dedication, and hard work. She discreetly requested her kind neighbor, Betty, to mail the letter for her. She promised to pay her as soon as JoJo sends her some money to use for her travel to the university. Betty knew her home situation, thus she consented to extend a favor for Shez. She guaranteed Shez that the letter would reach its respective destination without issues. And that was that. The promise was sealed with a sisterly embrace as Shez completely fell into an emotional acceleration. She displayed her weakness through tears, copiously covering her sweet brown eyes and sobbed. Betty comforted her like an older sibling, and a few minutes later, they parted ways.

The most awaited day had finally come as Shez eagerly got up and got ready to leave at five-thirty in the morning. She heard the rooster *cock-a-doddle-doo* loud and clear. She listened to the chirps of the hummingbirds in the garden that she maintained daily. The sunrays slowly crept by the maid's quarter's window, and the milkman just left the gate where three bottles of fresh milk patiently stood. She excitedly dressed herself casually, woke the other maids up, and bid them adieu. No further words were uttered. The three other maids quietly assisted Shez with her two pieces of worn-out luggage and carefully opened the gate for her to exit.

As Shez exited the house where she was maltreated and tortured for ten years, a single tear was captured, falling from her pale cheek. For the last time in her young life, she felt free and on her own. Mary and her relatives were aware of her departure, but they didn't care. No goodbyes were said, no financial help was offered. No hugs. Absolutely nothing. She felt the independence that she longed for the longest time and yet nervous and tense on what the future held for her. She prayed so hard for guidance and protection as she was about to navigate a big, cruel, relentless world in front of her. Slowly yet surely, Shez took her final steps to freedom with her quick little feet and began to breathe the fresh air of excitement and enthusiasm in the gigantic outside world, singlehandedly. She finally moved forward to independence as she kept these words in her mind.

And in that moment, I was broken
into tiny little pieces.
And yet I was fearless.
And was utterly alive.
I AM ALIVE, I AM FREE! I AM WHOLE AGAIN!

Shez arrived at the bus terminal right on time, bought a one-way ticket at the ticket booth bound for the city of her university. She sat at the back quietly and noticed passengers started to arrive one by one until the big bus was filled. It was loud and chaotic, early in the morning. But when the bus conductor blew his whistle, silence met the crowd, and everyone soundlessly started to settle in their respective seats and prepared for a long trip down a rocky, dusty, and bumpy ride of their life.

The bus slowly left the station and on its way into a rugged country road. The ride was truly bumpy and dusty under the unrelenting heat of the friendly sun. The passengers napped as the speeding bus entered the heavily packed highway. Shez took a book out of the bag and started reading it. Occasionally, she looked out the window to see fascinating views past the running bus. She was partly entertained seeing beautiful sceneries along the way, and, sporadically, her thoughts took her back to the house where she called a temporary hell on earth. The experiences she endured in that residence were events that she decided to forget to be able to move on. She had totally forgiven Mary and the rest of the relatives who made her young life unbearably contemptable. She couldn't help but cry mutedly and covered her wet face with an old scarf given to her by her good friend, Claire, from her high school days. She often thought of Jazmine as to where in the world she was. She thought of Claire as to what college she was attending. Then her mind wandered toward her family that heartlessly fell apart like a struggling wounded eagle flying toward a space called oblivion.

After several hours of traveling, the bus finally arrived at its destination. Shez was exhausted and starved. She got out of the bus and looked for a place where she could get a bite. She found a food truck where she purchased a chicken sandwich and a bottle of water. She ravenously devoured the food as she sat on top of a rock, under a huge tree. She needed to catch a cab to take her to the university. The cab ride was a short fifteen minutes, and then, finally, she found herself standing in front of an enormous campus ground of the university. She was amazed as she stood in awe of the vastness of her new bright world. She felt like a tiny dot enveloped in a massive yet mesmerizing landscape of the campus ground. Everything was beautiful and calm. The atmosphere was serene and conducive for learning. It was fascinating. As Shez looked around in awe, she noted that it was almost dusk, and there was not a lot of students around. And because it was only the enrollment period, only a few students were seen walking past her. Chaos and pandemonium have not yet occurred at that time.

Shez hurriedly asked people for direction to St. Bernadette's ladies dorm. It was at least a good thirty-minute walk from where she was. She was too tired to hike and was starved and exhausted. Forward she went with her two worn-out luggage in tow, patiently and good-naturedly. Her little painful feet walked slowly yet deliberately without complaint. She walked and walked and walked until she saw a very beautifully landscaped building from a distance. Her strode went quicker this time. It was already dark, past 6:00 p.m., and she needed to check in before the dorm closed. She kept walking until she landed on the front door of the dorm.

Carol, the caretaker, welcomed her with a sweet smile. Carol was a jolly, elderly lady in her seventies and very accommodating. She assisted Shez in checking in and took her to her assigned room on the third floor. The room was light and airy with a friendly ambience to it. Shez immediately felt comfortable as she started unpacking her few old clothes from her tattered luggage. She finally had a single room she could call her own, and no Mary or Lizette to boss her around. She suddenly realized the love and blessings bestowed upon her by her loving heavenly Father. She knelt to pray and gave thanks for the tender loving mercies and grace she received that very blessed day. She swiftly took a nice warm shower after she was fed by the dorm caretaker and suddenly found herself asleep in her comfortable warm bed without doing any tedious chores at all.

She reminded herself time and time again that she no longer lived at the torture house and that she was lifted by the grace of God. A light grin was manifested on her sweet face as she stared at the ceiling and whispered a soft goodnight to herself. Her tired good night unsaid.

Shez woke up early the following day, eager to start the day. It was a quiet morning as she witnessed the awesome sunrise from a distance. Her room window was facing east, and that meant watching sunrises every morning will be a common denominator for her daily activities. Birds happily chirped on top of a mahogany tree, right by her window. She likewise heard street sweepers' conversations, other students' footsteps toward the kitchen, and a faint classical music played from the lobby. Shez pinched herself to make sure she wasn't dreaming.

"Am I really here and not at my Auntie Mary's house?" She couldn't believe her good luck. She finally tasted freedom and independence, away from the toxic environment where she suffered so much for the longest time of her life. She was adamant to forgive and forget the entire miserable chapter of her life and ready to move on and start anew. Her excitement filled the air as she prepared to meet new friends and learn more about her new home. She carefully stepped out of her room and cheerfully trod toward the dining hall. She was greeted by the kind caretaker, Carol, and introduced her to other residents of the dorm. Everyone was so welcoming and friendly, and Shez quickly felt comfortable mingling with her new family, so to speak. She had a hearty breakfast together with her newfound friends and bid them adieu once done. She went back to her room to gather her school stuff and prepared herself for a long and exhausting day ahead.

Shez stepped out of the ladies' dorm and navigated the big campus with a map given by the caretaker, Carol. Her first stop was the registrar's office, made sure that she was registered for the freshman courses, met some professors and staff members and, most importantly, met the librarians at the old-fashioned yet huge library adjacent to the dean's office. She likewise visited the prospective classrooms for her upcoming classes and tried to focus her daily schedule as to where and what to prevent tardiness. She did well on getting to know the university and was ready to attend classes by the following week. She had a full-time student schedule, and her plans of working part-time was not accommodated at all.

The schedule was tight, and courses looked demanding and hard. She needed to maintain a certain grade to continue her academic scholarship, thus her idea of working part-time didn't pull through. Somehow, someway, JoJo, her oldest brother, managed to send her allowance for as far as he can afford. We must consider JoJo at that time was married with children of his own. His salary as military personnel was just enough to support himself and his family, and Shez totally understood his position. She was grateful for her brother by any means and counted herself fortunate to have such a thoughtful and caring sibling. She was careful with money and wary on budgeting. She catered for the needs versus the wants on her expenses. She learned this concept years ago when Mary didn't provide any allowance for her needs in high school. The hardships she experienced under Mary's guardianship taught her many things about life. Her struggles and hardships were her number one teacher when it came to living fully and not just merely existing. Shez wanted to thrive well, despite many obstacles that came her way, and she was determined to obtain success, no matter what happens.

She was deep in her thoughts but was interrupted by a soft hello coming from her left side. She turned her head and was mesmerized by this very good-looking young man grinning at her.

"Hello, I'm Dan. Are you new here? Freshman?"

"Ah, yeh. I'm a freshman. Oh, by the way, my name is Shez"— as she extended her hand to Dan. They shook hands, and together sat in a corner spot, outside the library.

"I'm freshman as well in the college of medicine," Dan articulated, and Shez immediately noticed his set of pearly, white teeth and winsome smile.

"I'm taking up law," Shez softly responded.

She thought Dan was the most handsome student she met that day. She was delighted and pleased. They engaged in a happy conversation for a few minutes until Shez excused herself as she hurried back to the library to borrow some books. Dan, on the other hand, merrily went his way. Shez, ultimately finished her university tour by herself, checked her prospective lecture rooms, met a few of her professors and classmates, met new friends, and met a freshman boy named Dan, from the college of medicine. It was a long and energy-draining day indeed.

The following week was the first day of formal school opening. Shez excitedly showered and hurriedly walked toward the dorm's dining room for breakfast. There were hellos and good mornings greeted by fellow dorm mates along the way, and she enjoyed the ambience and camaraderie of everyone. There were peace and friendliness manifested in the atmosphere which she loved, and Carol, the caretaker, was motherly to all. *Such a wonderful place to be*, thought Shez as she sipped her hot coffee with a sugarless creamer on it. She took some quick bites on the bagel and scrambled eggs, and off she went to the university.

Her first class was political science, followed by English, then economics for the morning session, and Shez was quite nervous and jittery with feelings of inadequacy in terms of knowledge as a freshman student. She calmed down as she reassured herself that she was there to learn and hopefully master what she had gathered. She knew where her first classroom was, so she was right on time as she walked into a room full of curious yet pleasant and eager faces. She took a seat in the second row and shyly opened her book and prepared for the professor's lecture. It was a couple of hours class, and the professor was so animated that nobody in the class felt bored. The lecture was interesting and fascinating. Shez's curiosity in political science paid off. She participated excellently in the discussion and quickly realized how much she loved the career she had chosen. She was now sure of herself that she wanted to become a lawyer, a great lawyer, and a champion defender for the poor, oppressed, and the innocent. She wanted to become a criminal lawyer in the future.

The first day of classes was quite long and tedious. She was overwhelmed with assigned readings, papers to write, activities to attend, and committees to join. She felt thinly stretched with homework to do and extracurricular activities to participate in. She sighed and comforted herself.

"*Don't stress out, Shez. You'll do well. Just let it be*," she justified herself.

Once again, she rushed toward the library, borrowed more books, and buried herself in assignments in a quiet corner of the law section. She softly turned the pages, attentively read each chapter, took notes on every essential information, and gathered all the facts for her paper. She was so focused on what she was doing and didn't even bother entertaining her growling stomach. It was almost 7:00 p.m. that she decided to head back to the dorm to get something to eat. She brought more books with her and wearily trod her way toward the place she called her new home.

The campus was still very much alive during that time. There were so many students who walked past her. She could hardly carry herself with the weight of the books in her hands. She just kept on walking. The ladies' dorm was approximately half an hour walk, and every corner was fully lighted. Her eyes tunneled toward the dorm, not paying attention to the noise and commotion of students that surrounded her. She finally arrived at her destination, ran toward her room to deposit the heavy books she carried, and happily rushed to the dining room for dinner. She then showered and prepared herself for bed. She was extremely dog-tired that she slept like a baby that night.

Her classes were in full swing, and Shez found herself in the middle of the first semester already. Soon, semestral break would come, and she was worried as to where she would spend it. She obviously didn't want to go back to her Auntie Mary's house of torture, and besides, she was not welcome there any longer. She was cursed before she left and gave her the final verbal abuse that her poor soul could hardly tolerate. It was a traumatic experience for Shez. She was totally bullied by Mary and her other relatives before she was let go.

They all gave her a warning of "once you leave this house, you are not welcome back anymore." And Shez had not forgotten those harsh words at all. She remembered everything. Her experiences were fully knitted in her brain that even in her sleep, she got nightmares out of it. She decided to ask Carol, the caretaker, if she could stay in the dorm during the semestral break, and Carol was fine with it. The only thing was that she would be on her own since everyone would go back home, and even Carol was set for a vacation. This meant she would cook, clean, and take care of the dorm (interior and exterior) while all were away. Shez thought about it long and hard, and because she had nowhere else to go, she chose to stay.

The first semestral break of the school year came, and every resident of the ladies' dorm was excited to take a break, except Shez. One by one left the place until it was only Shez and Carol and the two other crew members. Carol gave her a list of things to monitor, to watch out, to pay attention to while she was away. Shez listened intently to every word and suggestion Carol gave her. The cook and the housekeeper will be out as well. This meant it would be Shez by herself, for two weeks until Carol, the cook, and the housekeeper would be back in just a few days ahead of the residents. Hesitantly, Shez took the dorm over by herself. She felt so alone and lonely when Carol and the rest bid farewell. She never realized how big the residence was until she stood in the middle of it. She heard her own echo as she sadly walked in the hallway, toward her room. It was like an enormous, empty world of its own where her mere thoughts of how to survive within fourteen days by herself played a major role. She was panic-stricken, but she managed to keep her cool.

"I'll be fine. My heavenly Father will protect and guide me," she softly told to herself. *"My Savior, Jesus Christ, loves me. I am a child of God. I am, I am,"* she continued to whisper words of comfort and encouragement as she slowly yet surely plodded toward the kitchen to make dinner.

Shez intently made it sure that everything was locked up after her. The gate, the main door, the back door, the side door, the windows, the patio and, most especially, her bedroom door. All the lights went off at exactly 10:00 p.m. (following the dorm rules) as she gathered herself together and got ready to sleep. She was so exhausted that falling asleep was not an issue. After she said her prayers, once again, by the grace of God, she slept soundly like a baby.

She woke up quite late the following day. The sun was already up and shone brightly, the street sweepers had likewise finished their chores, and the entire outside world was as calm, peaceful, and serene as the inside of the dorm. There were hardly any people seen walking or jogging or running at the quadrangle, except a few gardeners and sweepers maintaining the landscape of the main plaza. She opened her window, facing the mahogany tree, and listened to the birds chirping away. She spotted a bird's nest with little ones noisily chirping for the mama bird with their beaks all opened, ready to gulp any worm that would come their way. It was a marvelous scene to behold. Shez chuckled as she watched the mama bird cater to the young ones lovingly. She thought of her departed mother at that very moment and, of course, her once-upon-a-time-happy-and-intact family. And because she had nowhere to go, she spent watching the bird family and other birdies for quite a while.

Hunger pangs made Shez jumped from her seat and rushed toward the kitchen to make breakfast. The dorm silently kept her company as she checked the pantry for any available food. The sound of silence inside the dorm was quite deafening. It was undeniably eerie and spooky without people's laughter and conversation that helped create a friendly vibe and caring ambience. There was indisputably no one around at all. She started to get goose bumps, hence, hurriedly inhaled the sandwich she prepared. She couldn't wait to get out of the building to change the ghostly feeling within her. She showered and changed and walked toward the library as fast as she could. Luckily for her, it was open.

Shez was warmly greeted by Minnie, the librarian who knew her from day one.

"Shez, you're here. When do you leave for home?' asked Minnie.

Shez responded with a smile, didn't say a word, yet asked Minnie for assistance in locating a political science book. Minnie did not hesitate to help and quickly found the book for her. Shez sat in her favorite spot and started reading the book attentively. She found the book interesting and fascinating. She was adamant that she made the greatest decision of pursuing law as her chosen field of interest. She was so focused on the book that she didn't realize it was almost twilight. Minnie warned her that she had a few minutes left till closing. The library closed early during term break, and Shez packed her things and bid goodbye to Minnie. She walked toward the ladies' dorm resignedly. *Time flies slower when you don't know where to go,* thought Shez as she just sighed.

"*Oh well, whatever,*" she snapped.

She was in the middle of the quadrangle when she heard someone called her.

"Shez, wait for me" were the words.

She turned around and saw Dan waving at her with a ball in his hand.

"Hi, Dan! I thought you've gone home for the term break," exclaimed Shez as she was charmed to see him. "How are you?" she continued.

"Shez, I have been looking for you since the day I met you, and for some reason, I can't locate you," Dan responded. "I'm doing okay. I'm not taking a break since I need to work on some projects for two of my classes," Dan continued as he wiped beads of sweat from his face.

"Oh goodness!" exclaimed Shez. "I'm so glad to see you. I live at St. Bernadette's ladies dorm. And you?" she resumed.

"I live in a flat outside the campus with some of my high school friends who are likewise enrolled in the college of medicine," Dan replied. "Can I help you carry your books? They look heavy," he smilingly continued.

"Sure, please do, and thank you so much," Shez reacted as she handed the books to Dan.

It appeared that both were so pleased to see each other again. As they reached the dorm, Shez unlocked the gate and opened the main door hesitantly.

"Well, thank you for walking with me," Shez uttered the words softly.

"Can I come in?" asked Dan.

"I would love to, but I can't. There's no one around but me, and I don't intend to break the rules," she responded as she placed her books by the door side.

Dan looked puzzled and confused, but he obliged. He had questions but chose to keep them to himself. He then asked, "Okay, can I at least invite you for dinner? There are people in the diner, which is situated a block away from here. Can we? Please?" he again queried.

Shez shyly smiled and responded with "Of course, I'll be happy to."

They settled in a cozy diner a couple of blocks away from the dorm. The receptionist offered them a romantic corner spot, gently lit, and with a gorgeous flowery centerpiece. A middle-aged lady singing a love song accompanied by a serious looking gentleman by the piano. The mood was calm and peaceful, and the place itself was quite empty, thus making it more romantic. A cheerful waiter approached them and took their orders. Dan ordered a margarita while Shez opted for a chilled mango juice. The appetizer came, which both gobbled and, of course, enjoyed the main entrée with satisfactory appetite. The meals were followed by chocolate cheesecake for Shez and strawberry ice cream for Dan. Their conversation contained mostly about school and classes. Dan was attentively entertaining and listening to Shez's stories and vice versa. They obviously had a great time spent together. This was their first dinner date after a few months of not seeing or talking to each other.

FIRST LOVE

To be in love for the first time is more than euphoria.
The feeling is suddenly magical. Every breath nicely
warms the soul. And all the senses excitingly soar.

—Chito Barrios

Dan took Shez to the dorm, right after their impromptu dinner date.

"Thanks for inviting me for dinner. I had a great time," she cautiously whispered to Dan.

"I absolutely had a blast with you. Thanks for accepting my invitation," responded Dan.

The air was fresh and cool. The atmosphere was serene and comforting. There was no one around them. Silence took over the poignant scene. Then they stared at each other gently under the expressive light of the muted crescent moon. The shadows of the front trees cascaded toward the two human beings whose eyes were only made for each other.

Dan tenderly gazed at her sweet face and murmured, "Good night, and take care of yourself. I'll see you in the morning."

Shez gave the sweetest smile as she echoed "good night" back.

Shez went inside the ladies' dorm happily as she locked the front door and trotted toward her bedroom. Her eyes twinkled with unexplainable feeling she felt deep within, and she prepared for bed.

"*Oh my God. I think I'm in love,*" she told herself while brushing her shoulder-length, black hair.

She warily opened her window, stared at the moon, which most likely stared back at her as she said, "*Dear crescent moon, thank you for*

71

lighting the world and mine. You are the only witness to what has trans-pired tonight between me and Dan. Please be mum about it for now."

She started humming a love song while Mr. Wind provided the cool, romantic breeze that kissed her happy face. She recalled a few of the lyrics of the song as she quietly sang a tune.

She impishly winked at the moon and carefully closed the window past her. After prayers were offered, Shez was on her way to dreamland.

Shez woke up quite early the following day, felt refreshed and rested. After breakfast, she started cleaning her room, the hallway, the kitchen, the dining room, and the outside areas of the dorm. She tended the garden that was in full swing with different kind of flowers. She was energetic, inspired, and motivated that she was able to tidy the entire building without getting exhausted. She sang during all these activities with soft music that played in the lobby. She was a picture perfect of a girl in love. But what about the boy in high school who was her biggest crush way back then? Was she still thinking of him? After all this time, Shez thought of the high school boy, occasionally, and wished to see him when given a chance, but unfortunately, it didn't happen. He was her puppy love whom she admired so much. He was the inspiration and the hope that made Shez the best version of herself, despite the miserable situation she was in. He was the reason why she pursued higher education and big ambition in life. Wherever that high school boy was, Shez had always kept him safe in her loving heart.

Right after cleaning the entire place, which took Shez half of her busy day, she quickly ate lunch and hurried to the library. In the same corner of the law section, she sat quietly while intently reading and taking notes for her term paper. Noiseless it may seem, but she got startled when Dan patted her shoulder.

"Hello there, good-looking!" he greeted.

"Oh, hi, Dan," she quipped.

"Mind if I sit beside you?" asked Dan.

"No, not at all. But just be quiet or else Minnie will shush us,"—Shez smiled.

Dan nodded and sat beside Shez with his book in tow. Both mutedly read, took notes, and tediously worked on their papers. Both buried themselves on their works with random glimpses between them. Sometimes, they glanced at each other, gave a smile, then back to what they've been doing. Time indeed was a culprit. Before they knew it, it was almost twilight.

"I just started, and it's time to leave already?" Shez softly spoke to Dan as she hesitantly looked at the big clock by the library's doorway.

"We're about to close," Minnie warned the students, and Dan and Shez hesitantly left the seats and decided to call it a day.

They got up and graciously bid Minnie adieu. They walked slowly toward the quadrangle, past some students playing at the plaza. They decided to get some pizzas at the university's kiosk. There were quite several students in the kiosk and passed the time with delicious fast food and sodas. The ambience was chaos yet fun. They chose a little corner where they ate pizzas hungrily. They shared a great conversation, and the noise and laughter of other students didn't really bother them. They appeared to be focused and attentive to one another.

"Shez, did I ever tell you how pretty and beautiful you are?" Dan bashfully revealed.

Shez felt blood rushed toward her face and blushed. She was quite embarrassed. She was speechless. All she did was shake her head.

"Well, I will tell you right now. You are the most good-looking girl I ever met in this campus, and I'm thankful that I saw you and got to know you first," he continued.

Shez stared at him tenderly and responded, "Well, I'm grateful to be your friend, and thank you for the kind words. This is the first compliment I heard from someone like you." And her face was as red as an apple and could hardly speak.

Dan held her hand tenderly, looked into her eyes, and said, "Shez, I don't know if this is the proper time and place to tell you something, but I hope that you'll allow me to."

Shez hastily shook her head and responded with "Dan, look at the sky! It looks like rain"—as she pointed up in the darkened sky, mostly covered with menacing nimbus clouds. "We better get out of here as quick as we can," she resumed.

"Oh, it's fine Shez. We're inside the kiosk. We're safe," said Dan.

"But, Dan," Shez retorted, "it's getting late. I need to go."

Shez was about to get up and run as fast as she could toward the dorm, but Dan stopped her.

"No worries, Shez, I'll take you home once it calms down. I promise."

Eventually, Shez remained in the kiosk until the unpredictable rainy weather cleared up. They continued talking about their classes and projects, plus papers due for the coming term, and once again, they looked like they enjoyed each other's company. The awful rain came to a clearing, and both walked toward the ladies' dorm. Silence took over while on their way. Shez shivered due to Mr. Wind's chilly breeze that crossed their way.

"*Thanks, but no thanks, Mr. Wind,*" Shez silently told herself.

Dan tenderly placed his jacket on Shez's shoulders, much to her surprise, but she took the warm jacket as a shield to protect her from the cold breeze and simultaneously thanked Dan for it. Once again, her heart beat so fast that she could hardly breathe. She was so in love with him but tried so hard to hide her feeling.

"I hate this stupid feeling. I don't know how much longer I can go on like this," she told herself weakly, and because of Mr. Wind, Dan didn't hear it.

When they reached the dorm, Shez unlocked the main gate, and Dan walked her toward the main door. A mild mist and drizzle continued. Shez hesitantly returned the jacket to Dan, who in turn told her to keep the jacket for the night.

"No, I can't," said Shez, smilingly. "You are going to need this on your way to your flat"—as she forcefully gave the jacket to Dan. "Look, it's still drizzling, and I want to see you tomorrow, healthy and happy as can be," she spoke.

Dan took it and stared at her one more time under a darkened sky and said, "Good night, my princess, sleep tight and sweet dreams. I will be here tomorrow morning to pick you up for breakfast."

And before Shez could say another word, Dan was already at the gate, waved his hand, and naughtily blew a goodbye kiss up in the air for her to catch.

Shez locked the door carefully and quietly, turned the lights on, and instantaneously threw her hands in the air, accompanied by "*Alleluia! Thank you, my God. Thank you.*"

She headed back to her room, unmindful of the stillness and the quietness of the big lobby, and once she reached her destination, turned off all the lights, except hers, and locked the door. Once again, after she showered and got ready for bed, she opened her window and checked the weather. The moisture continued, the cold billowy Mr. Wind abruptly kissed her face and caressed her hair, but she didn't mind a thing. Her thoughts were so pre-engaged with the time she spent with Dan. It was so memorable. How she wished to keep his jacket, even for the night. She could have slept with that jacket under her pillow. She was madly in love with him. And she knew that Dan loved her as much as she did. But the time was not yet. She knew. The time will ultimately come, regardless of circumstances. She went to bed after offering her prayers and gratitude to God. And hoped to arrive in dreamland with Dan by her side. And in a few minutes, she was on her way to la-la land.

A week passed, and Shez was excited to see Carol, the other crew members, and the rest of students back in the dorm, very soon. One more week to go, and she wouldn't be alone anymore. She counted the days for them to get back, and the dorm would be a happy place once again. She was thrilled to finally be able to invite Dan inside the dorm to visit her. She tended the garden when she heard Dan's voice.

"Shez, good morning to you. Can I at least come into the garden. I'm a good gardener, you know," he teased.

She hurriedly ran toward the gate and let him in. Dan gave her a bouquet of roses that made Shez's face blushed like a crimson red tomato.

"What's this for?" she quipped.

"For you!" Dan responded.

Shez was speechless. She fumbled and stumbled. She was excitingly panicked. She took the bouquet, smelled the roses, and softly whispered, "Thank you."

Their eyes met. Oh, how they twinkled. And out of nowhere, Dan found himself kissing Shez tenderly, of which she reciprocated. Two hearts beat rapidly like lightning. Both startled and backed off from each other.

"Oh, Shez, I'm so sorry," cried Dan. "I lose control and…and… and… I love you, Shez! I really love you so much." He was teary-eyed, and his entire body shook lightly. His face blushed, and his whole being trembled. Shez, on the other, ran toward him and kissed him once more.

With tears in her eyes, she exclaimed, "I love you, too, Dan"— as she started sobbing.

They both cried as they hugged each other. It was an emotionally charged yet romantic tender moment. They were all alone in a garden full of blooming flowers with butterflies, bees, and dragonflies who witnessed what had transpired that very morning. Mr. Wind danced away that made all the plants sway gently. Dan tenderly wiped her tears as he led her to a garden bench nearby. They sat like two lovebirds as Shez rested her head on Dan's masculine shoulder. They both quietly listened to the music playing inside the hall that Shez turned on earlier, prior to tending the garden.

Both were lip-synching to the words of the music that was played. So tender. So magical. Alas! Shez, after all the misery and agony she experienced growing up, she finally felt at peace with herself and with God as she held Dan's hands and leaned on him meekly and lovingly. They were in the garden for quite a while then decided to grab something to eat for dinner. Shez hurriedly locked the dorm's door and gate, and together with Dan, they happily strode toward the university's kiosk, past the quadrangle. Dinner was now more meaningful, and excitement was literary in the air. They only had eyes for each other as they ate the food they ordered. Shez told Dan that he was welcome to visit her in the dorm, since the residents and crew will be back in a week's time. Dan was even more excited about it.

Carol, the caretaker, the cook, and the cleaning lady came back and, two days after, the dorm started filling up with its residents. Chaos, fun, laughter, and loud conversation came back, the kitchen area got hectic, the dining hall was fundamentally occupied all day, and the slamming of doors more pronounced. Shez was so excited and satisfied seeing everyone come back. The dorm was finally back into the full swing of things. The new term had, indeed, begun.

BITTERSWEET

Life can be full of contrasts, of sweetness and sorrow.
Pleasurable today, regrettable tomorrow.

—*Chito Barrios*

Shez and Dan promised to love and respect each other as their relationship blossomed. They focused on their respective studies and spent their time together as needed. They dedicated their full attention and energy to the success of their chosen field and understood the time needed for the extracurricular activities they participated in. They supported and inspired each other. They were each other's critic and advocate. Both were very intellectual and driven. Nonetheless, both relied on each other's strength and love in whatever circumstance they were in. Dan comprehended Shez's situation financially and continuously inspired her to be her best version, especially in academics, to maintain and keep her scholarship. He wanted her to be successful in all her undertakings in the university. On the other hand, Shez tried her best to be a great soulmate to Dan. She had shown full understanding and love, regardless of any condition. Their partnership and love worked so well that the entire campus was aware of them.

One year, during their sophomore year, Shez got a big surprise. While she was busy conversing with friends at the dorm's lobby, Carol, the caretaker, privately summoned her and took her in the private room where her auntie Em waited. Shez could not believe her eyes.

Why is my auntie Em here? What does she want? She had so many questions in her mind while she approached and embraced Em.

She had not seen her for a long time. Both hugged each other with tears in their eyes.

"Auntie, so happy to see you!" Shez exclaimed as Carol excused herself and left them alone. "How are you, and what's up?" Shez continued.

Em was mum then cried. "Your grandmother passed away last week," Em replied. "She had a heart attack. We took her to the hospital, and she passed away there. Her body will be interred next week. I came here to let you know," Em sadly commented.

Shez was shocked. She felt awfully sorry for her grandmother's passing. This was the woman who beat her to death almost every day of her life, way back when. This was the woman she called Grandmother, and in return, she called Shez "the child of a criminal." The traumatic memories commenced in her mind as Em continued talking. She didn't hear her auntie Em's sad story at all. Her mind was consumed with old, fragmented recollection of a miserable, agonizing life she once had with them. Shez was silent and unremarked. Her sad emotions slowly turned into a hardened animosity that just resurfaced from the core of her very soul. She slowly backed off from Em, and with a sterned facial expression, she softly said, "I'm very sorry for your loss, Auntie Em. But, truthfully, it is none of my business. Besides. I have been very busy with school and had no time to attend her funeral. Please extend my heartfelt sympathy and sincere condolences to everyone involved, and thank you for coming all the way from your place to inform me of the news. May her soul rest in peace, wherever she's now," she ended the conversation by turning her back, away from Em.

Her auntie was left baffled yet not ready to give up. She chased Shez and said, "How could you be so cold? Where are your manners? Your family values? This is your grandmother! Her blood is in you. It's flowing strongly within you. Where is your gratitude?" Em was furious and agitated to witness Shez's reaction toward the sad news.

Shez went back to Em, and this time, intense and formidable, with tears falling from her eyes, she calmly yet gravely responded, "Grandmother? When did she become my grandmother? Have you ever known of any person called their granddaughter a child of a criminal? Have you? Were you ever beaten by a wooden stick almost every day, even when no wrong was committed?" Shez cried as she continued.

"Were you ever slapped with unforgiving words, day and night? I didn't mind the physical pain, but the words thrown at me hit directly to my heart and soul like sharp darts that battered my entire being in grief!" She pointed to her heart as her face blushed. "Auntie Em, have you or anyone of you taken the time to consider that I'm family as well? Those bitter moments are still here"—pointing to her heart—"I forgave her, Auntie Mary, Lizette, and everyone else in the family, but, unfortunately, I'm still unable to forget. I'm a work in progress, so to speak, and I fervently ask God every night to help me heal and turn this tragedy into a learning experience during my lifetime," she further stated.

Shez sobbed uncontrollably that her face was all red and wet while Em was left speechless. She then slowly backed off, turned away from Em, closed the door, and left Em without a word. She walked toward her room past the lobby, still sobbing yet firm and, without any sound, closed her room and retreated.

It was already late in the afternoon when Shez was awakened by the dining hall's loud bell, ringing for dinner. She was hungry but too weak and sorrowful to eat. She hated the fact of what had happened that day. She loathed herself for standing her ground. She despised her guts and courage. She detested everything about her today. She was inconsolable, devastated, and brokenhearted. She decided not to eat that night. She stayed in bed, not touching her schoolwork, not responding to Dan's numerous calls, and simply cried herself to sleep.

Shez woke up early the following morning. Jumped from her bed, showered, prepared for school, and went into the dining hall and hurriedly inhaled her breakfast and off the door. Carol, the caretaker, stopped her by the gate.

"Shez, are you okay? What happened last night? Your auntie left very upset, and you were not responding to Dan's calls. Are you all right? Do you want to talk about it?" Carol interrogated her like a professional detective.

"Thanks for your concern, Carol, but I don't want to talk about it. I'm sorry," Shez responded.

"It's fine, Shez. Take good care of yourself. Dan was very concerned." Carol ended the conversation and allowed her to go.

Dan met her at the quadrangle with a puzzled look. Their gaze met, and they hugged each other. Shez started tearing up.

"Shhh… You're fine. I'm here," reassured Dan as he hugged her tighter.

Shez continued to sob until her tears subsided. Then she slowly told Dan what had transpired the day before. Every bit of it, and because Dan was already aware of Shez's past life, he couldn't help but sympathize with her. He didn't say a word. He just stayed by her side, listened intently without judgment or comments. When Shez recovered from the emotional wreck of experience, both decided to get a bite in their favorite diner, which was just a couple of miles away from the dorm. Both ordered Italian and ate with gusto. They were starved; hence, the quick bite turned into a hearty meal with dessert and all. They were so into each other when, out of the blue, a sudden pat on Dan's shoulder.

"Hi, Dan, remember me?" A young, pretty girl was seen standing with a big grin on her face.

Dan looked up and smilingly said, "Of course I remember you!" as he stood up and gave her a quick hug.

"This is Shez, my girlfriend." And turning to Shez, Dan said, "This is Beth. My classmate in high school."

Both girls shook hands with warm greetings as Dan invited Beth to join them.

"Oh, thank you, but I just had my lunch. I was at the end corner when I saw you and Shez come in," Beth responded.

"I must go. See you around the campus, Dan."

"Wait," Dan snapped. "You attend college here?"

"Why, yes!" Beth answered back. "I'm taking up nursing here."

Beth quickly exited the diner while Dan and Shez resumed their eating activities. They enjoyed the strawberry sundae ice cream and banana split for dessert and remained engaged between themselves. They eventually left the diner, headed for their respective classes as they kissed and bade each other adieu.

Dan met with Shez right after classes, and both headed for the library to work on their paper and project. Minnie, the librarian, assisted their needs as they continued their homework. It was almost library's closing time when both decided to call it a day. Dan looked tired and beat up. He lovingly and dutifully walked Shez to the dorm. They were exhausted and sleepy as they walked past the quadrangle, where it was quiet and serene, and the full moon gave its light generously while the countless shining stars above kindly guided the sweet lovers toward their destination. As they reached the main gate of the dorm, Dan tenderly kissed his ladybug good night, accompanied by an affectionate hug, then they whispered goodbye to one another. Shez slowly and quietly closed the gate and the main door, turned off the lights past her and off she went to her room without any delay. She prepared for bed, offered her gratitude prayers to the Lord, opened the window quickly as she allowed Mr. Wind's cool breeze to touch her face and caress her hair. In a few minutes, Shez was in her usual dreamland place where she and only she could access it without any interference.

The following day came quickly. It was an exam day. A very busy day for students at the university. Shez felt ready for anything as she ate her breakfast and conversed with her dorm mates animatedly. She had a good sleep the night before and felt rested and prepared for anything that came her way. Suddenly, she found herself walking toward the campus, together with some of her friends. That day came quickly. Shez took the exams in the morning, had lunch by herself, and more exams came in the afternoon. She thought she hit all the questions correctly and was adamant to obtain excellent marks as a result. She was eager to reunite with Dan that afternoon when, suddenly, a classmate from the criminal justice course came her way.

"Hi" was the greeting.

Shez looked up surprised yet managed to smile. "Oh, hello, Bry! What's up?"

Bry looked gloomy as he responded, "It was a hard exam, wasn't it? The chapters that I focused on didn't come out in the exam. Quite devastating."

"Oh, C'mon, Bry. Don't be upset. You'll be fine. Let's wait for the results positively with fingers crossed," Shez reassured him kindly.

"Shez, you're so kind. Thanks for comforting me. I admire you, really. Brilliant! Kind! Humble! And beautiful!" Bry said with a twinkle in his eye.

"Well, not really, but thank you," Shez responded coyly.

Bry stayed by her side as they wholesomely conversed when Dan arrived at the scene. Shez immediately introduced Dan to Bry, and the two gentlemen shook hands, then Bry exited the scene. Dan was agitated and stressed at this time. He was not pleased with what he saw. He didn't want anyone conversing with his girl, let alone by themselves and without his presence. Dan hesitatingly expressed his opinion to Shez, of which she was not delighted about it.

"Dan, Bry is my classmate in criminal justice course, and I see nothing wrong talking to him. He's a sweet guy and a friend," she reasoned out.

"Shez, trust me. Bry is in love with you. I'm a guy, and I know," Dan quipped. "His body language tells everything, and I don't want to see you talking to him or do anything, whatsoever," he continued.

"Dan, please be sensible. It's you that I love. We are soulmates, remember? I don't want you to get stressed out about a thing that doesn't exist!" Shez tried to assure him.

"Shez, if you want to be my girl, you have to do what I tell you," Dan snapped back.

"Dan, I'm not your property. I have my own rights. Respect and trust are essential parts of a successful and healthy relationship!" cried Shez. "I am so disappointed in you, Dan. I can't be in a relationship with someone who distrusts and disrespects me," she continued with tears in her eyes. "There is nothing going on between me and Bry. Nothing."

Dan was quiet. Silence enveloped the two lovebirds. Neither broke the stillness within them. It seemed like an invisible wall was slowly building up between them, and they were helpless about it.

After a few minutes, Shez got up and slowly stepped out into the openness of the universe alone. She prayerfully expected for Dan to chase her and ask for forgiveness. Unluckily, there was no Dan beside her. There was no one to hold hands with. She felt partially paralyzed, incomplete, and utterly solitary. There were tears in her eyes as she kept her pace, further away from her first love who, at this point, walked toward the opposite direction from her. Shez kept walking toward the dorm, wiped her tears away, and tried her best to put up a happy face as she reached her sanctuary. She knew at that time that her relationship with Dan had gone kaput. Wrecked. Ended. Finished.

It was already dark when she finally retired in her room and prepared for bed. She had paradoxical feelings of happiness, just because exams were finally done and, at the same time, sadness because she missed Dan. She kept thinking why Dan behaved incoherently and illogically. There were times that she longed to receive a phone call from him, perhaps? Or a surprise apology visit? But, sadly, she never heard anything from him anymore. He was gone like a bubble that got pricked by a pin, and then *boom*!

"Losing a loved one because of a silly reason was incomprehensible. Bry was there for academic discussion, not to profess his love to me! Dan was being insensible and pointless. How can someone get jealous of a relationship that doesn't exist?" whispered Shez to herself.

Once again, she opened her window, facing the mahogany tree, and allowed Mr. Wind's cold breeze to sway away her hair and touch her warm face that instantly soothed her worries and comforted her fears. And in a few minutes, she was on her way to her beloved space where she was accepted and loved unconditionally, the dreamland.

Shez woke up early the following day and prepared for school to meet up with professors regarding test results. She was thrilled, at the same time nervous.

"Well," she assured herself, *"whatever happens, I have God by my side."*

Shez knew all along that God would never abandon, judge, or neglect her. Nonetheless, abandonment, misery, and struggle were not new to her. She felt like she was brought into this world to experience sadness and suffering to savor the sweetness of victory at the end. She reached her classroom in the nick of time since the professor was already giving out the test papers with marking on it. The professor called out her name as the topnotcher where she scored brilliantly with only one mistake that was questionable and could be corrected should she dispute it. The entire class applauded, celebrated, and congratulated her. With humility, she accepted the applause and thanked everyone for being kind and that her heart was full of gratitude for every blessing (great and small) that was bestowed upon her. Bry hugged her as she teared up during an unforgettable, happy moment with her classmates.

Shez yielded excellent results in all the courses she took that year. She maintained her academic scholarship and remained a full academic scholar in the university for the following year. When that remarkable day was over, Shez sat by the quad, alone, looking at the horizon. She reflected on her life—past, present, and, of course, the future. She witnessed the sunset by the west side of the quadrangle and sighed and quickly wrote an intense poem:

> *Let not your dreams dread.*
> *The coming of sunset!*
> *For sunsets are just but a quick rest*
> *To a promising sunrise.*
> *That will bring back hope,*
> *Of a wonderful ray of sunshine*
> *Kissed by a mesmerizing laughter*
> *Of one's soul filled with sweetness and ever after.*

She wished Dan was by her side and celebrated her achievements together. She thought of her broken family: her father, her brothers, especially JoJo whom she had not heard from for quite a long time now because of his work. She terribly longed for her family. She missed her departed mother. She ached for her old childhood friends, especially Jazmine. She wondered how Jazmine would look like at that time. Her mind was gripped with many things that she loved to have and to keep but arbitrarily lost them. Then she started sobbing.

"I don't know why I always end up alone," she whispered to herself. *"I always lose people I treasure and love. What have I done to deserve this, O Lord? Tell me, I pray, that I may mend my ways,"* she continued.

She felt so broken and vulnerable. Her heart ached and was torn into tiny, little pieces, yet she appeared stoic and fearless. She was vulnerable and weak deep within, just the opposite of her outward appearance that manifested intelligence and confidence. Slowly, it was dusk! The sun had set with its soft light that illuminated from a far distance. Suddenly, her wondering mind unwillingly positioned itself into the reality of life. She paced her footsteps heavily toward the dorm, where chaos and laughter from its residents filled the atmosphere. They were all ready and excited for summer vacation that had just begun, and for sure, it would be just Shez who would be left behind to manage the entire building. She joined in with dorm mates, smiling. Nonetheless, her heart was simultaneously broken. They all congratulated her excellent achievement academically and threw an impromptu party at the dorm for her, which was headed by Carol.

Shez's heart, despite being shattered, was filled with gratitude and humility. She was speechless for the appreciation given her by her dorm family. She joined in with the crowd as everyone socialized, ate, sang, and danced to their hearts' content. It was indeed a joyous night to remember. The celebration concluded around midnight, and when the lights went off, everyone slept like a baby.

Everybody but Shez and Carol, the caretaker, left the dorm for summer vacation the following day. Carol left the place a couple of days after. That left Shez by herself, who was used to the setup already. She wasn't scared and looked forward to a summer part-time job she got as an assistant librarian at the university. Minnie, the librarian, hired her since the library still gets busy during summer days. She started her job immediately while chaos took over the girls at the dorm as they tried to exit. Minnie happily met Shez at the library and gave her a quick orientation to the place. Shez quickly learned the routine and shared her excitement to others as she eagerly assisted them. She was engrossed and immersed with the responsibilities given and was surprised to see how fast time went by.

"Shez, it's your lunch break," reminded Minnie.

Shez looked at the wall clock and replied, "Thanks, Minnie. On my way."

She took her sandwich that she made at the dorm and her water bottle, and off she went outside the patio to feel the sunshine touch her face. There were no people around but the gardener. She settled quietly at a corner and ate her lunch when she saw a silhouette of a man from a distance. As the man came closer, she recognized that it was Bry.

"Hello, Shez," he greeted.

"Hi, Bry, why are you still here?" she asked.

Bry sat in front of her and explained that he needed to do some school projects and papers to write, thus decided to stay for the summer. Bry lived at the apartment complex a few doorsteps away from Dan's.

"Do you like your summer job?" Bry asked.

"Yes. I love it. Keeps me busy," Shez responded.

"I'm happy for you. You always seem to fit in any given situation. And you excel in everything that you do," Bry stated.

Shez blushed as she quickly finished her sandwich. "I need to go back to work. Thanks for dropping by." She then hurriedly went back in.

It was already dark when Shez clocked out and left the workplace and hiked past the quad, toward the dorm as fast as she could. It unfortunately poured rain that time, and she literally was soaked yet ignored it while Mr. Wind blustered her whole being. She never felt so alone and unloved that very moment. She felt useless and abandoned. The scenario was mentally and emotionally depressing, but she had to keep going. She had to. She wanted very much to live and not just exist in the cruel world. Her footsteps were steadfast and quick. The environment was eerie and dark, and there was no one in plain sight, plus the rain got harder as she tried to catch her breath and her tracks. From a distance, she could see the dorm's steel gate with a little light on that somehow assisted passersby to safety as they trod. Shez reservedly smiled as she approached her refuge. She couldn't wait to drop dead in her own warm bed.

She quickened her strides for as long as her body tolerated it. And in a few minutes, she found herself inside the dorm, and once again, just by herself since Carol had already left for her much-needed vacation. She ate a sandwich she made and ran toward her room. A prayer of thanksgiving and gratitude with a plea for protection and forgiveness was dedicatedly uttered before she bid the world her sad good night. Her good night was gloomily left unsaid.

She awoke early the next day, after a deep slumber, and impulsively prepared for work. She walked so fast to catch up the time. She hated the fact of reporting late for work, hence did her best to clock in on a timely manner.

"Good morning, Minnie," she greeted with a lovely smile on her face.

"Shez, did you make it home before the rain last night? I was thinking of you when the rain poured," Minnie asked her with a concerned face.

"Oh, I was soaked, but I made it fine," Shez replied as she continued to fix the books in the shelves.

"Oh, good to know. A student named Bry called for you a few minutes after you left last night. He wanted to give you a ride," continued Minnie.

Shez didn't say anything. She kept on working as she ignored Minnie. Minnie didn't think much of it. She likewise was busy fixing the magazines and books found on the other side of the library. It was past lunch hour when something caught Shez's eyes in the corner of the north wing. To her surprise, Dan and Beth were seated side by side as they softly whispered into each other's ears, gazed at each other lovingly, and they seemed to be taking notes from the books in front of them. There was a deep painful prick in her heart that made her nauseous. She felt a knife stab right into her four-chambered aching heart.

She was extremely hurt that she felt pain, yet she remained solid, cold, and unmoved. There were no emotions shown whatsoever. She continued working but wished that lightning would strike her soon. She literally just wanted to die. She lost a sense of purpose in life at that very moment. She felt betrayed by someone she truly loved and adored. She hastily went to the staff bathroom where she poured her deepest emotions to no one by sobbing as she lamented to God, "*Why, my Father in heaven, why?*" She was very distraught as tears flowed down her cheeks. "*Why is this happening to me? What have I done to deserve this? I have been in misery for a long time, and yet you continue to make me suffer!"* she continued while bawling.

The bathroom door silently opened. It was Minnie who witnessed the scene and instinctively hugged Shez like a mother hen who was prepared to comfort and protect her chicks.

"There! There! Hush now. Everything will be all right. Dan is not the only man created here on earth," Minnie said as she comforted her.

"There are many men out there who crave for your love and attention," Minnie tenderly comforted Shez as she dried her tears of agony.

Shez continued to shed silent tears as she composed herself, and together with Minnie, she cautiously went back to work. The time went fast as both neatened the library at the last hour, and ultimately, they clocked out and bade each other goodbye.

"Listen, go straight home and rest. Tomorrow is another day, and everything will be fine," Minnie reassured as she hugged Shez and exited the building.

It was getting dark, and the stars were in array, gallantly illuminating the galaxy and brightened her path toward the dorm. Her strides were lengthened. Her heart continued to hurt. She sighed as she occasionally wiped her tears of sadness. She wanted to reach the dorm immediately and hide herself from the cruel world. She felt that the entire universe was against her. She felt forsaken and unloved. She was halfway past the quadrangle when she heard someone called her name.

"Shez? Is that you?" It was Bry who slowly approached her.

Shez hesitantly stopped her tracks. "Bry? What are you doing here? It's getting dark. You should be in your flat already," she responded.

"Well, nothing! I just thought I could walk you home," Bry uttered as he scratched his head.

"Bry, please! Don't invest your precious time on me. I have no time for this. I'm focused on my studies and my future," Shez said with a straight face that didn't show any emotions at all.

Bry persisted, "I know that you and Dan are no longer together. Can you at least give me a chance?"

Shez looked at him and replied, "All right! Walk me home tonight, and then that's it! My priorities have shifted, Bry. No more love for me until I'm ready."

Bry grinned. "Okay, Shez. Just tonight. And, oh, by the way, I am willing to wait for another twenty years until you're ready for me."

And both laughed as they pressed forward, past the quadrangle, and toward Shez's destination.

Shez was surprised to find out that Bry was a very funny guy. They conversed and laughed all the way toward the dorm. She forgot her problems and sadness for a moment until Bry bade goodbye. He made sure that she arrived safely and was obviously elated with the opportunity of walking side by side with her, even for just a moment.

"Hey, Bry, thank you"—Shez smiled and waved back at Bry—"I appreciate you today. Thanks again." And she softly closed the gate and the main door of the dorm.

She rushed toward the kitchen to make a sandwich and hurried to her room and prepared for bed. She was exhausted physically and emotionally that she didn't have the energy to open the window for Mr. Wind's breeze to kiss her face. She dropped dead and slept soundly.

She was off the following morning, and this meant cleaning the huge place by herself. She ate a big, hearty breakfast, turned on the music, and started her chores. Unmindful of the noise outside, she concentrated on tidying the main hallway and the kitchen, dining hall, then the garden. She sang and danced with the music, occasionally, and appeared cheerful despite the unpleasant scenes that happened last evening. Her day passed by without a hitch and without any drama. She finally decided to move on with or without Dan. She needed to pay attention to herself first, her future, her studies, and her achievements and success.

THE SWEETER SIDE
OF HEAVEN

*My main priority in life is to be with my loving wife and
our son forever. And together, we can explore the universe
without reservation, we can live in the sweeter side of
heaven, while here on earth and stay happy always.*

—Ferdinand A. Perez

Time flew quickly like a lightning bolt that traveled across the
big sky in a blink of an eye. Days and months passed by, and
Shez's sophomore and junior years manifested happy, unforgettable
moments mixed with sorrows and struggles, and yet she managed
to always come out victorious and maintained her academic standing exceptionally well in the prestigious university. She was noted to
be the most popular coed in the campus, and her relationship with
Bry was even wonderful and awesome. Bry became her best friend
forever in daily life. Bry was always there for her as she was for him.
They enjoyed each other's company in a platonic manner. Bry acted
like a big brother, ready to protect her in any way he could. They
called each other "soulmates," respected, and loved one another, and
because they belonged to the same college of law, Bry was her constant companion in every activity they went to. On rare occasions,
Shez wondered how Dan was doing, but other than that, the loving
and caring feeling for him was kaput. She moved on without hesitation and enjoyed it. She hardly saw him since he was in the college
of medicine campus, and Beth was in the nursing college, so maybe
they got married already or who knows?

"*Dan is past,*" she sadly reminded herself all the time. "*He deserves Beth, and I hope that they are happy together,*" she uttered.

She focused on her courses, specializing in the criminal justice branch, buried herself with many extracurricular activities like the debate club, community outreach program, and the Thomas Hobbes Society. All the boys in the college of law wanted to date Shez, but she closed her heart for now. All the girls wanted to be like her—beauty, brain, kind, humble, and a hard worker. She remained approachable and grounded as she managed to support herself financially through part-time jobs offered by the university. She likewise continued to take charge of the ladies' dorm every term break, in between her works at the campus.

Shez and her oldest brother, JoJo, were in communication on occasion, and there were two occasions during her college days when he came to see her and bonded with his baby sister. Those were sweet memories that Shez cherished so much and was very appreciative with the opportunity to see her brother sporadically. She had not seen her Auntie Mary or Em and even cousin Lizette. And she dared not think of them either. She made herself busy as much as possible as she concentrated on her career and future.

One lazy afternoon, as Shez rested and napped in her room, she was abruptly awakened by a soft knock at the door. She answered the door and saw Carol, the caretaker, who mischievously said, "Oh my, Shez. There's a drop-dead gorgeous boy looking for you with roses in his hands."

Shez was half-awake as her brown eyes went wide with "What? What did you say?"

Carol replied as she pulled Shez toward the closet, "Go change. Fix that hair, and come down."

Shez obliged, and in a moment, she was on her way toward the visitor's area and was shocked with what she saw. Her eyes were wide open as she exclaimed with disbelief, "Benji? Is that you?" She shyly went toward him and shook his hand.

Benji was her biggest high school crush that didn't speak with her up until now. He was her puppy love in high school who unknowingly served as her inspiration and motivation to bring the best version of herself, despite challenges and hardships. He was the boy who gave her secret glances and enigmatic smiles but never spoke to her at all. His name was written all over her notes and in her teenage diaries, and he was the boy whom she admired the most, and yet it was only Claire (her high school best friend) who knew how much she loved him. And out of the blue, here he was, standing in front of her with a bouquet of pink roses in his hands. She was surprised. She pinched herself several times to ensure she wasn't imagining things.

"Hello, Shez! Thank goodness you still remember me. I have been looking all over for you and so glad I finally found you," Benji responded as he handed Shez the bouquet of roses. "This is for you."

Shez took the flowers and smiled softly. "What brought you here? And how did you find me?"

She invited Benji to the patio, and they awkwardly started their casual conversation.

"Shez, first of all, I want to apologize for being aloof and shy during our high school days," Benji started the ball rolling. "I was so embarrassed and immature at that time. I hope you'll give me a second chance. I'm not sure if you're still single and available. I'm just trying my luck at this point," he continued as he turned his teary eyes away from Shez.

Shez couldn't believe what she heard. Was it for real? Or was it a dream? She spoke softly yet clearly, "You are always here with me"—pointing to her heart—"You actually never left. Thank you for coming back. I have waited for this moment to happen, and here you are, making it a reality," she cryingly responded.

Benji saw those tears and lovingly wiped them as he whispered, "I will never leave you again. I promise. I have loved you since high school but was stupid enough to let you go. I love you so much, Shez. Please forgive me. I'm here, mature and responsible enough to protect and take care of you. You are the only one for me. I never loved anyone so much in my life. Please, Shez, give me another chance," he begged with teary eyes.

Shez reached out for his hand, squeezed it tight as if telling Benji that she was always there for him. They hugged and cried as they savored the sweetest moment of their life. It was Dan whom she considered her first love, but Benji was honestly her true love. Her biggest high school crush rekindled into a more serious relationship she ever experienced in her lifetime. They engaged in a serious yet intimate conversation while Shez's dorm mates left them alone in the patio. The flowers were in full bloom and danced to a tune of Mr. Wind's soft, cool breeze. The sky was radiantly blue as the sun shone on their happy faces. Birds chirped and sang as if they knew what was happening between the two lovebirds. The ambience was calm and serene, so romantically poignant that made them feel they were the only humans living in the sweeter side of heaven.

"Benji, just so you know, I had a boyfriend during my freshman year here in the university," Shez confided. "We broke off, and it has been two and a half years now that we have not seen one another," she continued.

Benji tenderly looked into her eyes and responded, "I'm a lucky guy. Thank you for saving that spot in your heart for me. I was so focused with college and never had a girlfriend before you. You are always in my mind for the past several years now."

"Oh, Benji, if you're lucky, I'm luckier than you," she said as she hugged him lovingly.

Both heard the music play softly at the lobby, and they hummed it together.

Shez felt so sure of herself that Benji is the guy she would marry. She felt it in her heart and in her entire being. Her heart was full of gratitude to the Lord as she was allowed to access the joy and the sweeter side of heaven. Her life journey was entirely a struggle for everything. She suffered so much as a young girl, endured many challenges and barriers while growing up, fought for things she felt were meant for her, and now she sailed away with the man of her dreams in the most blessed way. She couldn't thank God Almighty enough. It was dreamlike.

They decided to go out for a romantic dinner that very evening. Carol, the caretaker, momentarily allowed Benji's luggage to be stored in the dorm's guest room as it was quite too late to find a place to spend the night. Benji and Shez were humbly grateful for Carol's kindness. Both dressed up and bid Carol adieu for the night out.

Shez was familiar with the area and suggested to Benji the Italian restaurant where she and Dan frequented before. It was a nice place where the ambience was calm, peaceful, and serene. The waiters were friendly, the food was fantastic, and the people were respectful and welcoming. They were immediately accommodated when they arrived and was taken to a corner nook where she and Dan used to dine. Shez didn't mind the spot at all. She had forgotten the previous painful chapters of her life and was excited to move on with Benji. They ordered some drinks, delicious appetizers, and great food entrées to beat. The mood was romantic and tranquil, the lighting was soft and mellow, and both were engaged and focused on each other. Then the music started to become soft and seemed to invite everyone to the dancefloor.

"May I have this dance?" Benji tenderly asked.

"Why, of course. I'd be delighted," Shez quickly replied.

Benji took her to the middle of the dancefloor and softly and lovingly held her as they slow danced.

Shez closed her eyes as she rested her head on Benji's broad, muscled shoulder. *Dan never asked me to dance before*, she thought. This was her first slow dance with the opposite sex, and she felt so romantically in love with this guy. Every word of the song was meant just for her and Benji. It was indeed a celebration of a rekindled puppy love that was emotionally suppressed for many years, up until now. And the love came back stronger, firmer, and has turned into a true love that was sincere, understanding, and true. Benji held her tighter, and as crowded as it was, they felt they were the only ones in the room as he reached for her lips and tenderly gave her a sweet, passionate kiss. The light was dim, the music sweet, and their emotions were sky-high. It was the most memorable night for Shez and Benji as they continued to enjoy each other's company, unmindful of other people around them.

They went back to their table when the music slowly ceased. They continued to converse in whispers, oblivious of the loud music that didn't modify their sweet tender moments together. After a few minutes, Shez excused herself and made her way to the bathroom. Just as she stepped out of the bathroom, a silhouette of a man crossing her way was quite noticeable. She stopped to allow the man to pass, but the figure halted in front of her.

"Dan?" Shez cautiously whispered.

"Hello, Shez. How are you? I unfortunately saw you and your new man," Dan snapped. "He's such a lucky guy to have you. I'm very happy that you finally have someone who loves you so much. I can tell by the way he looks at you," he continued as he gazed into her bewildered eyes.

"You saw us?" she looked astonished. "Were you here before us?"

"Yes," he responded with a sorrowful look. "Can I hug you at least?" he begged.

Shez hugged him quickly and tried to get off the way, but Dan continued talking, "Shez, it didn't work out for me and Beth. We're no longer together for more than a year now. I tried to forget you and was unsuccessful. I wanted to get in touch with you again, but I always see you and Bry together."

"Bry is like my older brother, Dan. He was one of my best friends in the campus. There was nothing special between me and him," Shez softly uttered. "Bry is actually engaged to a beautiful girl as we speak."

Dan looked surprised after Shez's revelation. He finally realized how wrong he was. He let her go for some pointless reason. He was irrational and refused to hear Shez's side. He acted conceitedly, thinking that he was always right and could never go wrong. Now he ended up with no one. Shez saw tears in his eyes.

"Dan, would you like me to introduce you to Benji?" she coyly muttered.

"So Benji's the lucky man," Dan countered.

"He was my high school puppy love, and we got back together again, just today, in a big-time way," she answered.

"It's okay, Shez. I wish you and Benji the best of everything that life can offer," said Dan as he finally gave an inch to let her through.

"Bye, Dan. I wish you all the best in life as well. Take care of yourself." She walked past him and happily went back to Benji's arms. She felt so lucky and fortunate as she lovingly squeezed Benji's hands when she reached their table.

She was delighted to finally have closure with Dan with no guilty feelings whatsoever. She was so prepared and ready to move on and start life anew with Benji.

The night ended up so well as they strolled under the moonlight, toward the ladies' dorm. They held hands and walked past the well-lit quad, past the tall mahogany trees as fireflies joyfully accompanied them to light their way. It was past 10:00 p.m., the weather was seemingly warm, yet the breeze was cool as it touched their faces and caressed their hair. The moon was full, and its light magically shone toward them as it followed every footstep they made in a lyrical and inspiring motion. They felt nature was protective of them in a very mystical way and, surprisingly, both loved it.

Carol, the caretaker, was still awake when they arrived at the dorm. Benji kissed Shez good night, and he followed Carol who showed him the way to the guest room. Carol then eventually settled down and prepared for bed as soon as everything in the big place was locked and safe for the night.

All were up early for school as Benji prepared to leave for the next city where he was a senior in the college of engineering. He promised Shez to visit as often as possible and to keep in constant communication when they were away from one another. Shez herself was graduating from the college of law. Nevertheless, they made sure their class schedule aligned for more bonding as they planned for their future together. It was a sad day when Benji kissed her goodbye. She never felt so lonely watching Benji as he disappeared from her view. Carol, as usual, reassured her that Benji was just a couple of hours away and that he was always welcome to spend the night in the guest room as needed. Shez expressed appreciation toward Carol as she hugged her goodbye and started walking toward the campus.

A few weeks later, the much-awaited time to reunite with her father and his second family finally came as planned. JoJo, her oldest brother, came to fetch her. She was excited yet scared. She wasn't sure what her reactions would be to see her father again, after those long years of separation. They rode a bus that took a few long hours until they reached the city where Shez spent her childhood with nostalgic memories. She was excited to see her beloved father, and she hoped that he was as ecstatic as she was. The meeting was casual. She saw her father aged so much. His face was wrinkled with sunken eyes that reflected either deep sadness or cool tranquility, his hair was grayed and thinned, almost going bald, and he seemed delicately frail with pale-colored skin, and yet his overall authoritarian look overpowered all the debilitated manifestations he had. And when Shez intently looked at him, he was indeed the father that she innocently betrayed in the past and left behind for a long time.

Shez thought that her father was sardonically good-looking, hatefully calm, ghostly dry, and amazingly expressive. She slowly walked toward him and submissively hugged her father whose arms extended open to welcome his prodigal daughter. Both cried and sobbed mutedly. Their emotions were sincere. They missed each other's presence so much, and the body language was crystal clear with the evidence that blood indeed is thicker than water. There were no dry eyes during that very touching scene.

"Forgive me, Papa," Shez initiated the conversation.

"You have been forgiven on the very same day you left us," her father replied with an old man's reassuring voice. "I thank GOD to see you back after so many years of yearning and longing! You have grown to be a beautiful girl, just like your mom," he continued.

"Thanks, Papa. I'm sure she's rejoicing in heaven to witness this wonderful reunion," Shez added.

Shez finally met the now-grown siblings, aside from JoJo, of course, her stepmother, and her half siblings. Their eyes were all glued on her. They stared at her adoringly and lovingly. Her half siblings embraced Shez like they knew her for a long time. Shez was indeed missed by everyone and vice versa. It was a joyous and blessed encounter with her father and his second family. A little celebration ensued where they sang, danced with loud laughter and giggles, mixed with tears of happiness. Shez was grateful to accept JoJo's invitation for a family reunion once again. The fun lasted till the wee hours of the morning. Then it was time for JoJo to take Shez back to her dorm. A long goodbye process eventually passed. Shez promised her father that she would be back, embraced everyone, and again, the sad goodbye was mutedly spoken as she and JoJo waved them adieu.

She slept most of the time during the bus ride, and she arrived at the dorm in time for dinner as she likewise bid JoJo goodbye and thanked him for organizing the best reunion ever that she had attended in her lifetime. One of her greatest wishes was finally fulfilled. *To see her father again was an achievement of a lifetime.* She expressed her deepest gratitude toward Almighty God who allowed her to access another sweeter side of heaven in a most emotional and endearing way.

The total exhaustion from the reunion and long trip gave Shez a very good night's sleep after a quick dinner. She woke up early the following day and prepared herself for school. She eagerly placed a call to Benji since she missed his call the night before. They lovingly spoke for a while, wished each other the best of luck since it was the final exam day for both, and promised to keep in touch once the exams were over and done. She then hurriedly trod toward the campus as she fervently prayed for assistance from the Lord.

"Dear God, please be with me today. I didn't really have time to review my notes last night, but I'm hoping that I'll do well in my exams," she softly prayed as she lengthened her strides toward her classes.

Bry was already in the classroom, reviewing his notes quietly when Shez arrived.

"Shez, how are you? Are you prepared for the tests today?" Bry was worried.

"Hello, Bry. I'm sure I am prepared, but you never know," Shez nervously replied. "I was too depleted to study last night. The family reunion was emotionally draining, and the trip was tiring," she further reasoned.

"You'll do fine. I'm sure." Bry patted her shoulder as a reassurance.

Both eventually stayed at a corner as they crammed over their notes without interfering each other's thoughts and concentration. The ambience in that testing room was intense and nerve-racking. The senior law students hardly moved and spoke. Their focus on their notes was real and deep. A pin drop could be heard from a distance during this delicate time. It was unreal. The time appeared to pass quickly as the professor requested to turn in the test papers. Reluctantly, Shez submitted hers, calmly yet anxiously. It would take another twenty-four hours to know the score. This method was the same with the other courses for the last term at the university. All other courses' final exams were taken and finished, and all the students had to wait for the scores and final grades, then on to the graduation ceremony.

Shez and Bry discussed the exams on their way to the dorm. Bry was kind enough to walk her past the quadrangle and left her safe and sound at the dorm's gate, then went back to his flat after they bade each other the best of luck and adieu. It was a busy and tiring day for students. Shez decided not to bother Benji at this time since he was taking his finals at his university as well. She went to bed and fell asleep shortly. She was awakened by a soft voice from the intercom, after a couple of hours slumber. It was Carol asking her to take Benji's call from the lobby. She jumped out from her bed, ran toward the lobby, and cheerfully picked up the phone.

"Hello, love, how were the exams?" was her initial greeting.

"It was brutal," Benji responded. "And yours?"

"It was maddening, I hope I did well," she snapped. "I miss you. When are you coming over?"

"Hopefully, tomorrow afternoon, after I get the test results. I plan to stay there overnight. Can you ask Carol for the guest room?" he asked.

"Sure, no worries. Carol doesn't mind at all, and besides, she likes you a lot," Shez replied.

"Awesome! I'll see you then. Meanwhile, take care of yourself and rest early," he advised.

"I will. I love you, Mr. Engineer," Shez teased.

"Bye, Ms. Attorney. I love you very much," he sweetly responded.

Both hanged up, and Shez merrily went to the dining hall to get something to eat and planned to call it a day. She was starved and ate a full hearty dinner, chatted with some of her dorm mates, then prepared for bed as soon as possible. She was indeed exhausted after all the tough exams she took earlier that day.

The following day came. The sun was shining brightly. Mr. Wind's cool breeze gently caressed Shez's face by the window. It gently blew through her hair, and the chirps of the birds accompanied the graceful sways of the mahogany tree that seemed to greet her a lovely day. Shez had a great relationship with nature, and her natural surroundings felt her friendly spirit in a heavenly sense. She was always in alignment with them in a strange yet angelic way. She spoke and hummed with nature, especially during her lonely days, way back when she was under Mary's wings. Nature, in return, reverberated and comforted her in approaches that only she could comprehend. Shez was ready for school as she went down to the dining hall to grab some breakfast. A bagel and a cup of tasty chocolate milk were enough for her to face whatever would come her way.

A disordered classroom full of talkative yet friendly students met Shez that early morning. Everyone was anxious and worried as they waited for the professor to come. An hour passed. The professor arrived, and names were summoned alphabetically, and test scores/grades were covertly disclosed. The same process was performed in other courses, until ultimately, the ordeal was over. It was over. College days concluded as the students prepared for the commencement ceremony, and lastly, the battle to pass the thing called "bar licensing examination."

It was late in the afternoon when everything was over, and Shez hurriedly trotted toward the dorm to meet Benji. As she passed through the quad, she saw Dan walk toward her.

"Congrats, Shez! Finally, college days are now but a memory," he greeted.

"Wow! Thank you, Dan, and congrats as well as you proceed for your medical postgraduate internship," she responded. "Are you taking your medical internship here?" she continued.

"Nope. I'll be going to the next city to do my internship for two years," Dan replied. "I'm so happy for you, Shez. Are you marching down the aisle soon?" he went further.

"Most likely. We're talking about it. There are still licensing exams to hurdle for both of us. We'll see what happens," she responded as she tossed her hair to the wind.

"Well, I guess this is goodbye!" Dan sadly muttered as he leaned forward to give Shez a hug.

"Bye," she softly whispered, and they parted ways. Dan stood still as he watched Shez disappeared from his view. Tears fell from his eyes silently, and his face turned crimson red as he felt so sorry for himself. He thanked God that Shez did not see him that way. He thanked God that he had the golden opportunity of having a diamond in the rough come his way yet was sad to see her go. Unluckily, both didn't know that this would be their last time to see each other during their lifetime.

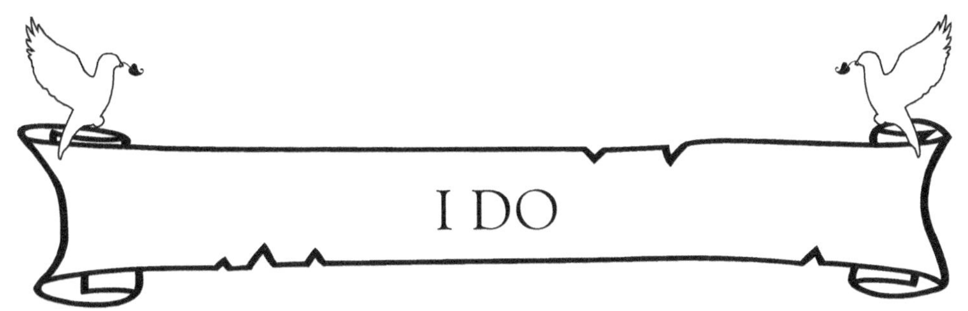

I DO

I only know one thing really, that when I see you, when I touch you, when the best part of my day is because of you, I am more content than I've ever been, and that will always be the only knowledge I need.

—Shez

Benji arrived at Shez's dorm around 6:00 p.m., in time for dinner that very same day. Shez assisted him to the guest room, and both happily stepped off the place to have a celebratory dinner at their favorite Italian restaurant. Both were thrilled that college was finally over, tests results were great, and the only thing that they must wait for is the commencement ceremony. Both likewise planned of taking the licensure exams as soon as possible and looked forward to a bright future together. Starved, they ate insatiably and only slowed down a bit when dessert was served.

"So when's the graduation?" asked Benji as he ate a tiny bit of the strawberry cheesecake.

"In two weeks. My papa is attending. It will be an ideal time for you to meet him," she responded excitedly.

"I like that. I look forward to the joyous occasion." He smiled as he tenderly touched her cheek.

"How about your graduation? When is it?" inquired Shez as she feasted on her chocolate with almond nuts ice cream.

"It's three days after yours. My parents will be there, and both are excited to meet you," he recounted.

Her eyes went wild. "Really? To be honest with you, I'm quite nervous."

"Don't be. I told them all about you, and they already love you. They are so eager to finally meet you in person," Benji reassured.

Shez got quiet. She was unsure how to react but calmed herself down when Benji held her hand. The hand squeeze was tight and reassuring. It was a feeling of confidence and comfort that he emitted to her whole being. It was protective and caring. She squeezed his hand back as she reciprocated his loving feelings. The moment was intense. It was a meeting of two hearts that beat as one. It was a warm sensation that penetrated two souls that were meant to be together in life. Shez finally realized that her knight in shining armor was here to stay, regardless of circumstances. He was hers, and she was his. They gently kissed amid people around them. That time, they were the only ones that truly mattered in the world. Just the two of them.

They left the restaurant and quietly strolled under the moonlight, past the swaying trees, toward the quadrangle. It was quiet and a bit eerie with no one around. Mr. Wind's cool breeze mutedly followed their every footstep without complaint, and the ambience was indescribable. Benji suddenly stopped walking, and to Shez's surprise, he was already kneeling in front of her with a ring in his hand. The diamond in the golden ring reflected as the moonlight tenderly touched it, making the diamond gold ring shine so bright amid the serene and still night.

"Shez," Benji whispered softly, "will you marry me?" His eyes were teary as mirrored by the light of the moon.

"Benji, I would love to. I would love to be your wife, and yes! I will marry you." She couldn't believe what she heard. She cried without hesitation. The moment was surreal. It was like a dream.

They hugged each other tight and gently kissed under several dancing trees as if to cover themselves from the moon who had been following them all along. Benji lovingly placed the ring on her finger, and she teasingly kissed the ring like no other.

"From now on, there's just you and me. I promise to be yours forever. I will be here for you to protect and love you, regardless. I will forever honor you, Shez. You are my entire world," said Benji, and he wrapped his arm around her as they continue to tread toward the dorm.

Their strides were slow, as if taking their precious time, savoring the moment together. Shez felt like a princess who finally found the handsome prince of her dreams. She felt like she was in fairyland with a magical moonlight lovingly hovering above them, accompanied by a friendly wind that was intentionally sent from heaven to provide romantic vibes that were profound and unforgettable. She felt the warmth of the atmosphere that had swathed them together. She sensed the cool air warily carrying them to their destination, and most of all, Benji's arm wrapped her entire soul with love that only they knew the magnitude of such emotion that was beyond words and comprehension.

> *I, I'm, I'm so in love with you*
> *Whatever you want to do*
> *Is all right with me*
> *'Cause you make me feel so brand new*
> *And I want to spend my life with you*

Carol opened the gate as they reached the dorm. She was quite worried but glad to see the two lovebirds safe and sound. She immediately showed Benji the way to the guest room as Shez proceeded to her own room. Sweet good nights were whispered, and Carol, the caretaker, peacefully and sleepily marched her way toward hers. All lights were off. The night was quiet. Nonetheless, Shez remained awake, looked out from her window, and gleefully watched the moon smilingly shine upon her sweet face, and the leaves of the mahogany tree continued to dance delightfully. She offered a prayer of gratitude to her Maker, and after a few minutes passed, she was on her way to la-la land.

What a beautiful sunrise it was when morning had broken. The sunrays signified hope and beauty that only an omnipotent one could create. The wonderful sound of nature gave everyone a reason to wake up and smell the roses. It was a day to behold. The sky was baby blue, the flowers bloomed, the morning scent was empowering and inviting that made the dorm residents come out to the garden and enjoy the heavenly scene. Shez went with her dorm mates outside as they enjoyed the purity of the fresh air provided by nature and had their happy faces touched by the rays of the morning sun. They realized that their days were numbered at the residence.

Sooner or later, parting time will be here, and most were graduating, hence the dorm would welcome newcomers by the opening of the new school year. They had mixed feelings toward the unfolding of the events for the week. Happy to be done with school and sad to say goodbye to a happy and nurturing place. They all participated to prepare the final dorm party that very day. Even Benji joined in. All had a specific task to do, and everyone seemed happy to be a part of the *"goodbye St. Bernadette ladies' dorm party."* Carol, the caretaker, was beside herself. She oversaw the event and worked so hard to make it a successful one.

The evening came, and everyone was dressed up nicely, ready to have a blast. The music was loud, the visitors arrived, the delicious food and dessert were spread out on a huge table, the drinks were chilled and ready, and by a quick review, everything was set for all to enjoy. Shez helped in the kitchen while Benji assisted with the tables and chairs in the dining hall as well as in the lobby. The celebration started at twilight. The dorm looked enchanted from the outside with all its colorful, dancing lights all around. The garden patio was romantically decorated, and the blooming plants and flowers helped create a serene and calm atmosphere. Everyone gracefully danced the night away with their partners, and this included the two lovebirds who were transfixed with each other. Benji wrapped Shez around his arms the whole night through, and both held hands like forever. They eventually went to the garden patio and, once again, allowed the moon to touch their loving faces as they gazed at the heavens.

"Look at the stars, Shez," said Benji as he pointed up in the sky.

"They look so awesome," Shez responded as she stared at the heavens.

"That's the constellation right there"—Benji smiled.

"Uh-huh. Mesmerizing. You know, I wish tonight will never end," Shez stated as she tenderly looked at him.

They gazed at each other affectionately, and Benji slowly reached for her lips, and both kissed passionately. The full moon secretly and shyly smiled in agreement to their expressed emotions. It floated toward the huge mahogany tree to dim the light and made the surroundings for the two lovebirds more private and sacred. They hugged as they whispered "I love you so much" to each other.

"Benji, Shez, come inside. Carol would like to say something," called one of Shez's dorm mates.

Both hurriedly went in and saw Carol in the middle of the crowd as she spoke with her teary, brown eyes.

"My friends, I am grateful to have the opportunity to know each of you. All of you are like my own children that I never had. You inspired and motivated me to be the best caretaker ever. I will surely miss you all and hope that you'll never forget me and this place. The world is your canvas, so go out there and find your purpose in life. Just remember to make our world kinder and friendlier in any way you can. God bless us and everyone."

The hall was overwhelmed with deafening applause. There were no dry eyes in the room that night. The dancing continued until it was time to conclude the fun. The party was a huge success, and it was indeed a night to remember for the rest of their young lives. When all the guests left the party, all the ladies, once again, pitched in to help the after-party cleanup and simultaneously bid each one a sweet good night. Suddenly, the lights quietly went off, and the tranquility and stillness of the night enveloped the magical place.

Shez's graduation day came. JoJo and the other siblings, plus their father, showed up to Shez's delight. Excitement was in the air. Benji finally met Shez's father, and a positive vibe ensued. Benji's parents were likewise in attendance. Benji made it a point that Shez met his parents on that special occasion. Optimistic emotions flooded their hearts as Shez stood in the pulpit to deliver her summa cum laude address to the graduates. It was right on target. She received a standing ovation applause for her speech.

"Fellow graduates, be prepared to explore the world. Take it with full humility and gratitude. And when you start to build your own empire, be silent about it. When you build in silence, your adversaries and competitors won't know what and when to attack. Silence is achievement's best friend."

She was on fire. She delivered her talk with all her feelings and energy. With all her heart, body, and soul. She was filled with wisdom that radiated from her miserable experiences and struggles as an abused child. She was maltreated by her own blood. There were no mercy and love in the household where she was trapped. And as a child who did not completely experience a parent's love, she thought her surviving father didn't love her. She fleetingly hated her father as the brainwashing occurred in the torture house of her relatives. She followed and naively trusted her maternal relatives. And there she was, unexpectedly betrayed by the people she innocently believed. *But there was Jesus! And there was a Father in heaven who never abandoned her.* Her unrelenting faith saved her from these ravening wolves who were dressed like lambs, yet calculatingly ready and shrewd to devour her. She strongly believed that God the Father and Jesus were always there to support and comfort her. God was with her from the beginning of her existence, and even now, she powerfully testified that God never left her side.

Shez concluded her speech where she could hardly see her audience. Her eyes were filled with tears, and the entire crowd was as silent as the well-behaved birds in the sky. Everyone cried. It was such a heartbreaking scene.

"I am forever grateful to my university who adopted, taught, nurtured, and loved me for who I am. To my professors, my classmates, my friends, and to all of you who touched my life, one way or another, I thank you. To my sweet father and my loving brothers, thank you for your love and support. To you, Benji, who loves me for who I am, please know that I love you. Thank you. To my Almighty God and Maker, and to my Savior, Jesus Christ, my humble heart and repenting soul, I completely offer you. I love you all, and thank you for everything. May God keep and bless us all."

Shez's speech touched and empowered everyone. Her father was so proud of her. He sobbed all the way till the end of the ceremony. She was extremely grateful for the opportunity given to her by the university. She considered it the biggest break ever afforded to her for free. She maintained her academic scholarship all the way through graduation. Humility and gratitude were her biggest weapons to achieve her dreams. And she achieved it with flying colors. And she made sure to let everyone know that her faith and belief in him made all things sweet and possible in the end.

Benji's college graduation came three days after hers, and once again, the two families gathered in celebration for Benji and Shez. Moments like these are unforgettable events that occurred in people's lives such as theirs. Success is not measured in the amount of money you make but in the number of lives you impact. One of the hot topics discussed during the celebration was the union of Benji and Shez. Both families agreed on the marriage, and a simple wedding ceremony was in the works that made the celebration event more meaningful and worthwhile.

After all was said and done, the wedding day came with Benji and Shez more in love with each other. Theirs was a love that kept growing in times of sorrow and joy. They planned of taking the licensure board exams together, although in separate venues. Shez focused on the bar exams for lawyers, and Benji concentrated on the electrical engineering exams. To avoid getting overwhelmed, both decided to take baby steps slowly yet surely. The wedding ceremony was simple with less than thirty guests, including families in attendance. Shez wore a lovely white gown that she herself picked from a department store, whereas Benji wore a white tux and white trousers with white, shiny men's shoes to match.

She looked so beautiful and angelic with a lacey veil that flowed along with the wind. Mr. Wind was always by her side, regardless of the activities. She seemed to float in the air as she nervously held her father's arms toward the altar where Benji waited anxiously. Wedding vows were tenderly said to one another:

Benji vowed, "Today and every day, for as long as I live, I choose you again and again. I am with you in times of happiness, sadness, success, failures, sickness, and in good health. It will always be you and me over and over again because I love you. You are a gift from God to me. You are my entire universe. To be by your side, I will always be."

Shez vowed, "Benji, you have been my love since high school, and up to this point, that little love of mine grew into a forever. I love you to the moon and back, always and forever."

Love was totally in the air during the exchange of vows, especially when both quietly, yet tenderly, exchanged their "I dos." Their wedding song softly played in the background after the priest pronounced them as man and wife as they lovingly kissed each other under the heavens.

The guests applauded and cheered the newlyweds, and off they went to celebrate the happiest moment of Benji and Shez as husband and wife. The wedding celebration was a success. They shared their wedding bliss with their families, relatives, friends, professors, dorm mates, especially Carol, Bry and his ladylove, and those that Shez managed to touch their lives in one way or another. The wedding party was held in the ladies' dorm's enchanting garden with Carol, the caretaker, in charge.

All Shez's dorm mates (some served as bridesmaids and maid of honor) were there and made the celebration more memorable. Everyone helped from the decoration to the food preparation and even entertainment. It was cozy, warm, and friendly. The ambience was serene yet jolly, the flowers were in full bloom that seemed to participate in the celebration, and the trees continued to display the dancing leaves as Mr. Wind loyally blew soft, warm breezes to the happy place. It lasted till the moon took over the post, which allowed the sun to set away and rest. It was indeed a night of jubilation. And to make the story short, right after a sweet goodbye was spoken to the family, friends, and guests, off toward the horizon they flew for their much-awaited lovey-dovey honeymoon.

EPILOGUE

Never judge the future of a person based on their present condition because time has the power to change any black coal into a shiny diamond. Shez's life journey is one of the greatest examples I know that proved the saying *"Life is like a wheel. Today, you're at the bottom. Tomorrow, you're on top."* It tells us we should not be discriminative of anyone's overall situation because everything here on earth is temporary. Shez faced many struggles during her lifetime, but as helpless and vulnerable as she was, she never gave up hope. Facing battles in life is never fun, but when you put on the armor of hope and relentless faith in God, there's no doubt that you can climb any mountain that blocks your way to happiness and contentment. You will not be neglected or abandoned *"if, in him, you believe."* Shez faced failures that caught her unprepared, but she turned around with all her might and strength and eventually conquered them all.

And just like any other true story, Shez's personal life journey ended up being happily married, she and her husband, Benji, hurdled their licensure exams without issues and quietly worked hard to establish themselves within the community they chose to live. Shez became a well-known defense criminal lawyer. She was fearless when it comes to justice—intelligent, articulate, with strong decision-making skills, sensible, super listening skills, confident, and totally involved. A year after graduation, she established her own office and quickly progressed into the ranks of the most-sought defense criminal attorneys in the city. She was unstoppable, relentless, and persistent.

Benji, on the other hand, became the city engineer. He was witty, skillful, possessed good public relations, and was a hard worker. Slowly, they grew massive in power and popularity as they helped the community progress into a most-pursued place to live. Nonetheless, difficult as it was, they ultimately decided to migrate to the Land of Promise, which is called the United States of America. They had a son born in the USA, worked so hard to establish their own practice, and contentedly lived there even to this day. Both are now peacefully retired, and both remained grounded and kind to anyone. Shez's sweet spirit shines within her, and I can see it manifested through her eyes. I sensed sincerity and humility as she reminisced about her journey in life, most especially her childhood.

She looked forward to meeting her departed parents (and parents-in-law) again in the afterlife. She has not experienced a true mother's love here on earth since her mother left when she was only seven, and she could only hope that she would feel her love once again when the right time came. She was otherwise deprived of growing up with her father, and she wholeheartedly yearns for him as well, even now. She told me, at one point, that she feels her departed father's presence in her life every day, and she's loving it. Shez remains in contact with her oldest brother, JoJo, who is a retired military, and some of her other siblings. She's adamant that her biggest regret in this lifetime was her failure to grow up with her father and siblings way back then. If she could only turn back time, she would, without a doubt. If she only knew then what she knows now, her entire life story would be different.

She asked for her father's forgiveness, several times. Nevertheless, her oldest brother, JoJo, assured her that their father totally and completely forgave her of everything. She surely has repented of the things she did to him, but who could blame her? She was just a child when the tragedy struck.

Otherwise, Benji and Shez had shown an eternal love for each other. They remained faithful to one another and openly declared that they were not just a happy couple. They were destined to be eternal soulmates as well. They have a happy family with their son who is also a high achiever. Their son is a successful doctor in the specialty of pediatrics, and both Benji and Shez can't wait to have their first grandchild play in their backyard very soon. Both are in good health and are enjoying the bounty of blessings they get from their heavenly Father each day.

As a good friend who knows Shez very well, I conclude that she never had any uncertainties about the unconditional love of the Lord bestowed upon her. She never failed to call his name, and she wasn't wrong. Her silent tears and desperate calls to him were always answered. The Lord God never deserted her at any given time and day. Shez indeed never walked alone in her lifetime. God walked beside her from the day she was born to earth and to this day.

Thank you for the time you invested in reading my book. I certainly hope that you enjoyed it and hopefully gained something worthwhile from it. May God bless you and your family always.

Sincerely,

Dr. Susie Angus-Perez

Acknowledgments

To Newman Springs Publishing team that specifically focused on my manuscript/story, thanks for assisting me with everything. The fruition of this book was made possible because of you. My personal passion in life is to write a book/books, and it came true, so to speak. I will treasure this forever. Thank you.

To Shez (not her true name), thank you for sharing with me your life story. Thank you for the courage and willingness to allow me to narrate the events of your life journey and share it with the whole universe. You are indeed a diamond in the rough who encountered many challenges and trials in life but ultimately witnessed the sweeter side of heaven and received God's bounteous grace. You are one of the blessed ones as you faithfully believe in *him*. May God bless you and your family always.

To my friends and family (Shez, Chito Barrios, Porferio R. Augus Jr., my oldest brother, Ferdinand Perez, my loving hubby), who shared with me their thoughts that I graciously quoted to make the chapters more interesting to devour—my unending thank you to you all. Continue being a joy multiplier for others. May God bless you always. So thank you once again.

A big thank you, once again, to my husband, Ferdinand, and our son, Fridrich Shane, who inspire and motivate me to become the best version of myself in everything that I do.

Lastly, I thank thee, my heavenly Father and my Savior, Jesus Christ, for the unconditional love, the many tender loving mercies, and the countless grace bestowed upon me and my family.

To God be the glory!

www.ingramcontent.com/pod-product-compliance
Lightning Source LLC
Chambersburg PA
CBHW022019150726
47990CB00002B/722